THE LIBRARY'S CRISIS COMMUNICATIONS PLANNER

A PR Guide for Handling Every Emergency

JAN THENELL

American Library Association
Chicago   2004

While extensive effort has gone into ensuring the reliability of information appearing in this book, the publisher makes no warranty, express or implied, on the accuracy or reliability of the information, and does not assume and hereby disclaims any liability to any person for any loss or damage caused by errors or omissions in this publication.

Composition by ALA Editions in Sans Extended and Minion using QuarkXPress 5.0 on a PC platform

Printed on 60-pound white offset, a pH-neutral stock, and bound in 10-point coated cover stock by

The paper used in this publication meets the minimum requirements of American National Standard for Information Sciences—Permanence of Paper for Printed Library Materials, ANSI Z39.48-1992. ∞

Library of Congress Cataloging-in-Publication Data

Thenell, Jan.
    The library's crisis communications planner : a PR guide for handling every emergency / Jan Thenell.
      p. cm.
    Includes bibliographical references (p.   ) and index.
    ISBN 0-8389-0870-5
    1. Libraries—Safety measures—Handbooks, manuals, etc. 2. Archives—Safety measures—Handbooks, manuals, etc. 3. Libraries—Security measures—Handbooks, manuals, etc. 4. Archives—Security measures—Handbooks, manuals, etc. 5. Libraries and mass media. 6. Crisis management—Handbooks, manuals, etc. I. Title.
Z679.7.T45 2004
021.7—dc22   2004010891

Copyright © 2004 by the American Library Association. All rights reserved except those which may be granted by Sections 107 and 108 of the Copyright Revision Act of 1976.

Printed in the United States of America

08   07   06   05   04   5   4   3   2   1

CONTENTS

PREFACE   v

ACKNOWLEDGMENTS   vii

1   The Crisis Communications Plan   *1*
When Emergencies Turn into Crises   4
Developing Your Crisis Communications Plan   4

2   Gathering and Maintaining Crisis-Ready Information   *7*
Ready to Respond   7
Gather Your Contact Information   8
How Will You Communicate?   10
Basic Library Information: What to Have on File and on the Website   11
To Do   12

3   Assembling the Team: The Collective Intelligence   *13*
Creating a Balanced Team   13
Makeup of the Crisis Communications Team   15
The Voice of the Library: The Leader-Spokesperson   18
The Importance of Speaking with One Voice   18
To Do   19

4   Identifying Library Audiences and Stakeholders   *20*
Identifying Your Library's Stakeholders   20
Maintaining Regular Communication with Stakeholders   21
Creating a Stakeholder Communications Grid   22

Educating and Nurturing Stakeholders   24
To Do   25

5 Assessing Your Library's Crisis Potential   26
Your Library's Annual Checkup   26
Conducting the Vulnerability Checkup   27
To Do   33

6 Creating Ready Responses for Areas of Vulnerability   35
Stay Ahead of Your Critics: Prepare and Practice   35
Crisis Response Example: Workplace Violence   36
Ideas for Talking Points   40
To Do   42

7 Building Positive Media Relationships   44
Working with the Media before a Crisis Occurs   44
Working with the Media during a Crisis   47

8 Communicating during a Crisis   52
The Power of Emotion: Messages with Feeling   52
What to Do Immediately   53
What to Do As Soon as Possible   55
To Do   58

9 After the Crisis: A Time of Opportunity   60
What People Hear, Believe, and Remember   60
After the Crisis   60
Conclusion: A Crisis Communications Success Story   63
Your Crisis Plan: A Work in Progress   64

APPENDIXES
1   TWENTY TIPS FOR WRITING AN EFFECTIVE NEWS RELEASE   67
2   SAMPLE NEWS RELEASE   69

GLOSSARY   71
FURTHER READING   73
INDEX   75

PREFACE

For many years, I was able to combine the best of two worlds: my position as public relations director for the Multnomah County Library in Portland, Oregon, and my nighttime-weekend hours as an adjunct professor of writing and public relations in the communications department at nearby Marylhurst University.

The communication readiness information I offer in this book (although certainly not all the crises I describe!) comes largely from that combination of learning experience. It's also the result of hands-on knowledge gained as a member of Oregon Governor Victor Atiyeh's press-communications staff and, earlier, as a news reporter supplementing my fellowship income during graduate school. But even before all that, I was an advocate for community libraries, serving two terms as library board chair in a small, rural community and more years as an urban library board member in Salem, Oregon's capital city. As I write this, I serve on still another library board, this time in Tigard, Oregon, where our medium-sized library is about to get a lot bigger, thanks to a progressive community that is building a new, much larger library despite the current ailing economy.

I have had the incredible good fortune to be able to learn from and work with two of the most visionary library directors in the United States—Sarah Long and Ginnie Cooper. Both understood—instinctively—the importance of using solid communication practices to lay a groundwork of community goodwill that could be counted on in times of need.

When Sarah hired me in 1986 to set up a public information office for Multnomah County Library's fifteen-library system, my years of politics, journalism, teaching, and library advocacy came together into what I thought then—and still think—was the best job in the world, one that melded my professional skills with my personal convictions.

Sarah's combination of determination mixed with southern charm set long-overdue changes in motion for Multnomah County. When she left to return to the Midwest, I found another kindred soul in Ginnie Cooper, whose vibrant energy, political savvy, and passion for libraries brought local, regional, and national respect to the Multnomah County Library System.

The structured approach of this guide is the result of all of the above. My hope is that it will help you prepare for the almost-daily emergencies and crises that beset your organization, no matter its size; that by completing the worksheets you will be able to more easily manage what may seem at first like an intimidating task; and that you will use this guide to help build a solid public information program—one that increases your organizational confidence and lowers your organizational stress level.

JAN THENELL

ACKNOWLEDGMENTS

To my friends and former colleagues at the Multnomah County Library, especially the best public relations staff anyone could ever ask for: Fred Ash, Eric Barker, Don Bradley, Terrilyn Chun, Pat Cozart, Joe Dressman, Dulsanna Eliason, and Jennifer Fox. A special thanks to June Mikkelsen, who patiently taught me about library culture and whose supportive friendship often made daunting challenges look doable. Thank you also to the library directors and consultants who generously allowed me to interview them for this book: Margaret Barnes, Ginnie Cooper, Carole Dickerson, Ed House, Sarah Long, Anne Prusha, Jim Scheppke, Dallas Shaffer, and Cecelia Swanson.

To my students at Marylhurst University, from whom I continue to learn.

And always: to Cathy, Ed, and Casia; Karen; Scott, Lesley, Griffin, and Andrew. Thank you all.

The Crisis Communications Plan

CHAPTER 1

In government, there is a direct and demonstrable connect-the-dots between how well you communicate and how well you govern. You may be handling an emergency in the very best fashion, but if you don't communicate that effectively, your organization can be seen as unresponsive, not in control, not caring. —Tim Reeves, former press secretary to Tom Ridge[1]

"Bomb left in front of Multnomah County building; police and firefighters evacuate the area round Division Street and Southeast 11th Avenue."[2] That headline of October 5, 2001, from *The Oregonian* caused more than a little apprehension among nervous Portland residents. Like the rest of the United States, they were still in shock after the terrorist attacks on the World Trade Center and the Pentagon. Fortunately, local FBI agents soon determined that an unidentified liquid found with the small pipe bomb contained no biological or chemical substance harmful to the public.

Even before the terrible events of September 11, 2001, directors of public organizations had been forced to acknowledge the awful possibility that real crises could happen in their buildings: natural disasters such as floods or earthquakes; man-made crises such as bomb threats or cybercrime; emergencies with the potential for assault or vandalism.

Indeed, the workplace has become a dangerous place. According to the U.S. Department of Labor's Occupational Safety and Health Administration (OSHA), some two million American workers become victims of workplace violence each year.[3] Violence consultants at Perelman Security Group estimate that about 1,000 workers are killed, 84,000 are robbed, and nearly 51,000 are raped or sexually assaulted each year. Another 400,000 are injured by aggravated assault, typically with a weapon involved.[4] Certain workers, says OSHA, are especially vulnerable:

- those who deliver goods or services to the public
- those who work alone or in small groups, especially during late night hours
- those who work in high-crime areas
- those who work in community settings where they have extensive contact with the public[5]

Those Who Work in Public Buildings—Such as Libraries

Libraries may have helped perpetuate the myth that "it could never happen here." To much of the public, libraries—like schools—are safe places, refuges from the world's violence. That's what makes the thought of a library or school crisis so repugnant. After the Columbine High School shooting, the manager of communications services for the Denver-area Jefferson Public Schools could only shake her head as she answered a reporter's question. "That this could happen in a school library . . . what could be safer than a school library?"[6]

The reality is that a library's very openness makes it vulnerable to crisis. Because we admit everyone, because our patrons are as diverse as our communities, because our hours extend into the night, because our buildings may be sparsely staffed or located in high-crime areas—in short, because we serve the public—we must be prepared to deal with events that have the potential for serious harm. We fear that our organizations are not invulnerable, that the events we read about and hope we never have to experience could happen in our towns and our buildings.

In today's world, how an organization handles a crisis will be remembered for years to come. Remember the Exxon *Valdez* disaster? It is a classic case of what *not* to do when a crisis thrusts an organization into the headlines. After the *Valdez* oil spill off the coast of Alaska in 1989, it was almost a week before the corporation's chief executive officer summoned the courage to face the press and the public. He didn't understand the importance of keeping the public informed about the extent of the damage, the environmental safeguards that were already in place, and what the company was doing to contain the spill. The result? The spill not only cost Exxon billions of dollars, but it also left its reputation in shreds.[7]

Events of much less magnitude than the *Valdez* oil spill can bring instant visibility to an organization. Given its generally positive reputation in the community, a library may be especially vulnerable to unwanted publicity. When a crisis occurs, early and frequent communication with patrons, staff, the library board, volunteers, the media, and the public is critical.

Would you be able to assimilate information quickly and accurately if one of the following real-life headlines happened at your library? Would you be prepared to speak out to protect your library's reputation even while taking any necessary corrective action?

- "Denver Library Patron Stabbed While in Children's Section" (01/21/02)
- "Man Arrested for Having Sex in Canadian Library" (01/14/02)
- "New Challenges Filed at Beleaguered Texas Library" (01/27/03)
- "Cold Weather Damages Pipes, Causes Floods in Three Libraries" (01/27/03)
- "White-Rights Speech in Pennsylvania Library Triggers Violence; 25 Arrested" (01/21/02)
- "Teen Melee, Gunshot, Raise Security Concerns in Savannah" (09/04/2000)
- "Binghamton Closes All Four of Its Branches" (01/13/03)
- "U. Penn Library Head under Inquiry for Child Porn Resigns" (04/21/03)
- "Christian Rights Group Sues over Nixed Library Meeting" (01/20/03)
- "Detroit Public Library Accused of Mishandling Grant Money" (06/18/01)[8]

What can you do now so that you'll be ready to act and able to communicate the reasons for your actions? How can you help your staff, your patrons, and the public stay calm in the midst of chaos, even when there is little information available?

The answer is to prepare *before* a crisis happens—to thoughtfully consider your organization's mission and create a communications plan in keeping with the values that define your place in your community. A communications plan (also called a public relations plan) is a vital component of any emergency action plan. In addition to doing everything possible to help any victims in an emergency, library officials and staff must continually respond to and reassure the public by sharing information about what has happened and what is being done.

A library's public relations responsibilities can no longer be defined by the traditional—and limited—tasks of publicity and promotion. Public relations efforts build positive working relationships between organizations and the people who have a stake in them. Using a mix of strategic planning and communications tools, good public relations practice creates a reservoir of goodwill that allows an organization to function effectively even in a crisis.

WHEN EMERGENCIES TURN INTO CRISES

Libraries across the country—large, small, public, school, academic, specialized—have been dealing with small-scale emergencies for a long time. Angry or disruptive patrons, latchkey kids, more users than computers, community decision makers who see the library as a "frill," others who would rid the shelves of materials they disagree with, disgruntled staff members who affect the morale of their coworkers—the list goes on. While most of the issues will remain relatively small in scale, they all have the potential to blossom into crises if left unchecked.

These everyday mini-emergencies provide valuable training for more serious occurrences. If the idea of preparing for a crisis seems daunting, think about how you've handled smaller incidents in the past. The principles are much the same.

A crisis is an emergency that has intensified. A crisis interferes with normal business, triggers close media attention, and can jeopardize an organization's reputation. To see how easily a library emergency can escalate into a crisis, consider these scenarios:

> Emergency: A child falls in the children's area, hits his head, and requires stitches.
> Crisis: The worried parent sues the library, charging inadequate or incompetent staffing.
>
> Emergency: An angry employee objects loudly to a disciplinary action.
> Crisis: An employee threatens or intimidates library staff and patrons.
>
> Emergency: An irritated patron objects to a library exhibit that he considers one-sided, obscene, or erroneous.
> Crisis: He assembles a group of like-minded citizens to campaign against future library funding.

Each of these incidents has the potential to become a larger issue that could endanger the library's reputation. With a solid crisis communications plan in place, your library can respond quickly to defuse an issue before it escalates. Your plan should include the elements listed in figure 1-1.

DEVELOPING YOUR CRISIS COMMUNICATIONS PLAN

A crisis communications plan is a structured way to think about how to communicate when the pressure is on. Its purpose is to avoid mistakes that can live on long after an emergency or crisis is over.

FIGURE 1-1 Elements of a Crisis Communications Plan

Designated crisis spokesperson
Crisis communications team
Crisis communications kit with contact information and library background information
Vulnerability checkup
Talking points for vulnerable issues
Guidelines for working with the media in a crisis
Post-crisis opportunities

Organizations like the American Red Cross know how important a good communications plan is in a crisis situation. That's why the Red Cross included a specially trained rapid response communications team with the early disaster relief volunteers it sent to the World Trade Center site on September 11. The thirty-five-member team was in place within half an hour of the first plane crash. Its job was to implement its crisis communications plan, working with the media to tell people what was happening and how they could help. When the huge volume of media calls swamped its offices in Washington, New York, and Pennsylvania, the Red Cross called in scores of volunteer professional communicators to help disseminate immediate information about relief efforts.[9]

It's not necessary to address every detail, but having a prewritten general communications plan gives you a head start at a time when hesitating to speak could be costly to your library's reputation. It doesn't have to be lengthy; when you need it, you can flesh out the details as they become known. The good news is that you won't have to go it alone in developing your communications plan. One of your first steps will be to create an ace crisis management team of library staff and others who are ready to provide help and support.

In this book you'll learn, step by step, how to identify sensitive issues that could spark negative publicity, how to create easy-to-understand explanations for each issue, and how to put in place the communication tools you'll need when emergencies arise. By gathering the materials and completing the exercises in each chapter, you will create a communications plan that is unique to your library. That plan will be a valuable tool for dealing with everyday emergencies as well as strategic preparation for a more serious crisis. You will have taken a giant step in preparing yourself and your library to communicate quickly in an emergency.

As you work through the book, you will assemble the elements of your crisis communications plan and you will add more items to the plan basics outlined in figure 1-1, including tips for working with the media, communication checklists to guide you through a crisis, and strategies for making the period after a crisis a time of opportunity.

While no crisis communications plan can prevent a crisis, good communications management can defuse the risk of negative publicity and even enhance your library's reputation in the community. The planning process itself enhances morale and allays fear. As library staff and others work together to recognize possible crisis situations, they develop strategies that give them a sense of control over what might otherwise be seen as totally unpredictable.

#

NOTES

1. Tim Reeves, in advance materials for National Summit on Strategic Government Communications. Reeves was scheduled to address the summit on Thursday, Jan. 31, 2002.
2. Norm Maves Jr. and Angie Chuang, "Bomb Left in Front of Multnomah County Building," *The Oregonian*, Oct. 5, 2001.
3. "Workplace Violence," OSHA Fact Sheet, U.S. Department of Labor, Occupational Safety and Health Administration, 2002. Available at: www.osha-slc.gov/SLTC/workplaceviolence.
4. "Creating Safer Places to Work," Perelman Security Group Inc., 1999. Available at: www.perelmansecuritygroup.com/psg_cspw.htm.
5. "Workplace Violence," OSHA Fact Sheet, U.S. Department of Labor, Occupational Safety and Health Administration, 2002. Available at: www.osha.gov/SLTC/workplaceviolence.
6. Alison Stateman, "I Didn't Know What a Crisis Was until April 20," *Public Relations Tactics*, April 2000.
7. Rich Long, "Remembering the Exxon *Valdez*," *Public Relations Tactics*, March 2003.
8. *American Libraries Online News*, 2002, 2003. Available at: www.ala.org/al_online.
9. Allan Houston, "Crisis Communications—the Readiness Is All: How the Red Cross Responded," *PR Week*, Oct. 22, 2001.

Gathering and Maintaining Crisis-Ready Information

CHAPTER 2

> *There cannot be a crisis before next week. My schedule is already full.*
> —U.S. Secretary of State Henry Kissinger[1]

In this chapter you will begin to assemble the basics of a communications kit that you can use every day, not just during emergencies. You will also identify key pieces of library information to gather for your files and to make available on your website.

READY TO RESPOND

Communicating concern and explaining how a crisis or emergency is being handled are part of a library's mission of service. In a serious situation, the first minutes and hours—indeed, the first 24 hours—are crucial. People want to know what's happening immediately. If no information is available, the rumor mill will fill the void.

Emergencies also seem to happen at the most inconvenient times—at night, during the weekend, over holidays. When the unexpected happens, you'll need up-to-date contact information immediately at hand for library staff, board members, reporters, and others. The sample worksheets in this chapter will help you start collecting that information now, when the need is not so urgent.

Keep your contact information up to date and carry it with you at all times. Ask key library administrators and crisis communications team members to do the same. Do not store the contact information in a large, three-ring notebook that sits on a shelf. Make it portable and easy to update. Enter the information into a computer file, copy it to CDs, synchronize it to a handheld device. Update it monthly. If these options are not available, print out, laminate, and distribute updates at least once a month.

GATHER YOUR CONTACT INFORMATION

Your communications kit should include contact information for library staff, crisis team members, library stakeholders, and the media. Your library may identify other groups as well. Assign a detail-oriented person to compile the data and keep it up to date.

Contact Information for Library Staff

Create contact lists similar to those shown in figures 2-1 and 2-2 to begin the first step of your communications kit.

LIBRARY ADMINISTRATORS

List emergency contact information, including phone numbers, cell phone numbers, pager numbers, fax numbers, and e-mail addresses of your library administrators. Include after-hours information.

FIGURE 2-1 Contact Information for Library Administrative Staff

Name:	Work phone:	E-mail:
Title:	Cell phone:	After-hours information:
	Pager:	
	Fax:	
Name:	Work phone:	E-mail:
Title:	Cell phone:	After-hours information:
	Pager:	
	Fax:	

FIGURE 2-2 Contact Information for Key Library Staff

Name:	Work phone:	E-mail:
Location:	Pager:	Other:
Title:	Fax:	
Name:	Work phone:	E-mail:
Location:	Pager:	Other:
Title:	Fax:	

KEY LIBRARY STAFF

List names, work locations, phone numbers, cell phone or pager numbers, fax numbers, and e-mail addresses for key library staff, including front-desk staff. Key library staff should be able to activate an in-place telephone tree, intranet site, or fax broadcast to the rest of the library staff.

Contact Information for Crisis Team

Once you have appointed a crisis team, you will add their contact information to your communications kit: names, work locations, phone numbers, cell phone numbers, pager numbers, fax numbers, e-mail addresses, and after-hours information.

Contact Information for Key Library Stakeholders

In future chapters you will add stakeholder contact information to your communications kit. Stakeholders are individuals or groups who have a common interest and a shared stake in an organization's success. Also called *publics,* or *constituencies,* they include members of your library's governing body, such as the city council, board of commissioners, or other funding authority; library board members; support groups such as Friends of the Library, library foundation, and library volunteers; and other community leaders. Keep names, phone numbers, cell phone or pager numbers, fax numbers, e-mail addresses, and after-hours information for these stakeholders.

Contact Information for the Media

Keep an updated listing of reporters and editors, names of their media organizations, phone numbers, cell phone or pager numbers, fax numbers, e-mail addresses, mailing addresses, and after-hours information as available (see chapter 7).

HOW WILL YOU COMMUNICATE?

Even while you are gathering the contact information, you can also be identifying the communications tools currently in place at your library. Examples include staff memos, intranet, news releases, the library website, information phone lines, board minutes, telephone trees, regularly published newsletters, newspaper columns, and community calendars.

Create a checklist similar to the one in figure 2-3. List the tools your library already uses and identify the staff members who are responsible for each.

FIGURE 2-3 Library Communications Tools in Place

COMMUNICATIONS TOOLS	RESPONSIBILITY OF	CONTACT INFORMATION
Staff memos		
Staff intranet		
News releases		
Library website		
Library board minutes		
Telephone trees		
Monthly/quarterly newsletter		
Newspaper columns		
Library/community calendars		
Other		

BASIC LIBRARY INFORMATION: WHAT TO HAVE ON FILE AND ON THE WEBSITE

You'll also need basic, easy-to-access information about your library—in print and on your website. Consider using fact sheets, histories, mission statements, descriptions of the library's governing structure, annual reports, financial information, information about library support groups, and thumbnail biographies of key library administrators.

Once this information is assembled (see figure 2-4), assign responsibility for keeping it current to someone who is detail oriented. Out-of-date information about attendance or circulation is of no use to a reporter who needs it in a hurry and could result in an erroneous news story that damages your credibility with the media.

FIGURE 2-4 Information to Maintain on File and on the Library's Website

COMMUNICATIONS TOOLS	WHO'S RESPONSIBLE	LAST UPDATE	ON LIBRARY WEBSITE?
Mission/philosophy			
Fact sheet/statistics			
Governing board members (use library's address)			
Directional map with locations, addresses, phone numbers			
Budget information			
Annual report			
Brief history			
Support groups: Friends of the Library, library foundation, others			
Biographical information: director, administrative staff			
Patron comments/questions/complaints: A log			
Other			

What to Include on a Fact Sheet

Your fact sheet should include usage statistics and information on the library's services.

- population served by the library
- number of cardholders
- annual circulation, other user statistics
- number of staff
- number of branches and buildings
- building addresses, phone numbers, open hours
- size and age of buildings
- a map showing the location of the library and any branch libraries

Now that you have gathered all the important contact information, the next step is to assemble a crisis management team, which we'll discuss in chapter 3.

TO DO

- ☑ Gather staff contact information and library background pieces; use the worksheets in this chapter to organize your information. Post the background information on your library's website.
- ☑ Designate a person who is responsible for keeping contact information current. Distribute updates to library administrators and crisis team members at least monthly.
- ☑ Create a staff telephone tree with several point people to receive breaking information. They will each contact three to five people, and they in turn will contact three to five more people, and so on. Test the tree the next time bad weather threatens.
- ☑ Using your library's basic web page design, create a hidden web page that can be fleshed out with information and activated quickly when needed.

#

NOTE
1. Henry Kissinger, June 1969, as quoted in the *New York Times*, Oct. 27, 1973, p. 32.

Assembling the Team: The Collective Intelligence

CHAPTER 3

A crisis situation calls for clear lines of authority; key people must be reachable all the time.—Ginnie Cooper, executive director, Brooklyn Public Library[1]

In this chapter you will identify the professional and personal skills that will be needed on your crisis communications team. Prepare a contact sheet like the example in figure 3-1 when selecting your library's team members.

CREATING A BALANCED TEAM

Now that you've gathered your contact information, the next step in creating your organization's crisis communications plan is to select a team of crisis managers. A well-coordinated team with a rapid response communication system in place will give you a head start at containing a crisis. The team's primary responsibility is to prepare for potential emergencies, including managing crisis communications with the library's staff, patrons, governing groups, and other stakeholders.

Selecting the right people for your team is critical. Many voices need to be represented, but the team should remain small enough to operate efficiently. The size of your team will vary with the size of your library, but more than a dozen members could become unwieldy.

Team members must possess a variety of skills and attitudes, the most important being their willingness to serve and their commitment to the library's mission of service. They should also have proven their ability to remain calm in stressful situations. It is especially important that they be highly intuitive and sensitive to how the library is being perceived by the public.

FIGURE 3-1 Crisis Communications Team: Contact Information

Leader-spokesperson:	Work phone:	E-mail	Stakeholder assignment(s):
	Cell phone:	After-hours information:	
	Pager:		
	Fax:		
Team member:	Work phone:	E-mail	Stakeholder assignment(s):
Job title:	Cell phone:	After-hours information:	
	Pager:		
	Fax:		

In addition to being able to work well under stress, team members should be problem solvers and clear thinkers who can take on whatever responsibility is called for, make decisions, work well with others, and meet regularly—perhaps quarterly—to practice what-if scenarios. When selecting team members, look for technical knowledge, comfort with ambiguity, ease with people, and endless patience with questions from reporters and the public.

Think broadly and inclusively; good team members are not always those with the most authority under ordinary circumstances. Consider your most patient reference librarian, the library assistant who has shown special skill in soothing upset patrons, the custodian who knows where everything is, the staff person who always knows how to get things done. Don't forget middle managers who successfully juggle the often-disparate concerns of their staff and their own supervisors.

MAKEUP OF THE CRISIS COMMUNICATIONS TEAM

The crisis management team is multifaceted, and each member plays a separate role. The following positions will form the core of your crisis communications team.

Library Spokesperson

The team leader will most often be the library's spokesperson. Because he or she plays a major role in making the crisis decisions that will influence the public's perception of the crisis and its management, the spokesperson will usually be the library director.

Primary responsibility: to serve as the voice of the library, speaking quickly, truthfully and humanely while preserving the library's good reputation.

Public Relations Manager or Adviser

Public relations professionals are the communicators, the people who have their finger on the pulse of the citizenry. They are ready to speak quickly on the library's behalf because they know the media—whom to contact, what to say, and how to say it effectively. They have established credibility with the media and other stakeholder groups.

Beware the temptation to delegate this critical responsibility to a library staff person just because he or she is good with people. It takes just one crisis to appreciate the media complexities that can confront the novice. If this is your only option, provide training as soon as possible. A better option is to ask local public relations practitioners or journalists to serve as volunteers or members of the library board. Even in larger libraries that have public relations professionals on staff, it is wise to have a list of local practitioners to call on in an emergency.

As a link between the library and the public, another important responsibility of library public relations is to make sure the library's proposed actions are in sync with its mission of service to the community. Public relations is a function of management. As such, it is the direct responsibility of the library director or her designee.

Primary responsibility: to facilitate and manage effective communication between the library and its users, staff, governing boards, and support groups, as well as the media and the general public.

Representative Library Managers and Staff

A library's staff people are its most direct link to the public. During an emergency, it's essential to keep information flowing (both ways) between library decision makers and front-desk clerks, telephone receptionists, website coordinators, and others. Be sure to include members of this important group on your team, and enlist their help in preparing communications methods and procedures. They can help to answer questions such as: Which library managers should be notified when an emergency occurs? What are the best ways to notify library staff when an emergency arises outside their work area? How will information be shared with library staff during a crisis?

Primary responsibility: to allay the fears of patrons and others by answering questions with information that has been confirmed by the library director or public relations office. Staff are also responsible for relaying the public's questions and concerns to library leadership.

Human Resources Director

The human resources director is the person most closely involved in the human factor during a crisis. He or she might be called upon to provide counseling, set up help centers, spend time with family members, or even notify next of kin.

Primary responsibility: to provide whatever humanitarian services the library is able to offer in an emergency or crisis.

Support Staff

The technical and clerical skills of library support staff will be vital in keeping information before the public via website, telephone hotlines, and written publications.

Primary responsibility: to distribute authorized information quickly and accurately to the library's website manager, telephone outlets, library publications staff, and communications outlets.

Building, Technology, and Operational Managers, Including Security Staff

Primary responsibility: To act as main information links between the disaster site, the information center, and the crisis team; also to manage the regular business of the library during an emergency or crisis.

Legal Advisers

The best person for this role is a legal expert who also understands public relations and public opinion. While it's essential to establish a good working relationship with your organization's legal counsel, remember that he or she does not have to answer to the court of public opinion or continue to lead the library after the crisis is over. Lawyers will counsel caution; it's their job. Be prepared to disagree if necessary, and manage for the long term.

Primary responsibility: to provide legal advice as needed.

Other Team Members or Community Partners

Eventually, you will identify others in your community that you want on your crisis communications team. These might include community service representatives from police, fire, emergency medical services, and other governmental agencies.

Primary responsibility: to coordinate the delivery of emergency services as needed.

Don't forget to select alternates for each team member. And at your first meeting, create a method for replacing members who leave the team. It may even be a good idea to write brief job descriptions for each member, as shown in figure 3-2.

Assure your team members that your library is committed to providing training and allocating staff time for emergency and crisis preparation. A good way to begin would be to hold a daylong planning retreat (see chapter 5 for a suggested agenda) followed by a schedule of work meetings. Once a plan is in place, check-in and update meetings should be scheduled annually or semiannually.

FIGURE 3-2 Sample Job Description

WEB DESIGNER AND WEB CONTENT MANAGER

Attend and participate in scheduled crisis team planning and practice sessions. Arrange for alternate if unable to attend.

With library director's office or public relations office, create plan to assure that information on the library's website is up to date at all times.

Design the template for a hidden crisis website that can be activated quickly during an emergency or crisis.

Create a plan for immediate web entry of authorized information should a crisis occur.

Create a staffing plan to enable constant updating of web information should a crisis occur.

THE VOICE OF THE LIBRARY: THE LEADER-SPOKESPERSON

If there is ever a time when an organization must mobilize itself to speak as one body, it is during a crisis. Remember the Exxon example in chapter 1? When the *Valdez* oil tanker ran aground in Alaska's Prince William Sound in 1989, company executives—lacking good information and with no clear communications direction—made inconsistent, even contradictory comments to the media. Their mistakes, along with other company blunders, engendered suspicion among the press and the public.

When one inside group contradicts another, however innocently, credibility suffers. The leader-spokesperson thus becomes *the* voice and symbol of the library during a crisis. Her office—or her designated public information or public relations office—becomes "information central." All information and information requests flow through this office.

As the public representative of the library during a crisis, the spokesperson must be a good communicator who understands the human need to hear concern first, reasons and rationale second. She must be an effective leader, an effective decision maker, and an effective speaker. She will have already established trust with the media and the public. She should possess good interview skills and be able to communicate well under pressure. She should be knowledgeable enough to speak easily about the crisis and about libraries in general. She should be a quick study, learning quickly from successes and mistakes.

Depending upon the scope of the emergency, others may also speak for the library, especially the public relations officer. The public, however, most often wants to hear from the "person in charge," and it is the director who can speak with the most knowledge, credibility, and impact. If the chosen spokesperson is someone other than the director, the initial statement to the press and the public should be made by a person who is perceived as *the* authority: the director, the library board chair, or the president of the library's board of governors.

THE IMPORTANCE OF SPEAKING WITH ONE VOICE

The anthrax scare that followed the terrorist bombings of the World Trade Center illustrates further the folly of failing to speak authoritatively with one voice. For days and weeks after the first anthrax letters were found, no clear, knowledgeable spokesperson emerged to provide credible information and allay public fears. As various agencies worked to get a handle on the scope of the problem, the public received a host of contradictory statements.

At the height of the outbreak, Secretary of Health and Human Services Tommy Thompson told television viewers that the government was prepared to deal with any kind of bioterrorism attack. Days later, it became clear that he had misspoken; government scientists had much more to learn about anthrax.[2]

Contrast the public's perception of the anthrax scare with the press coverage of New York Mayor Rudolph Giuliani's actions after the terrorist attack.

> For weeks afterward, Giuliani was more than just a mayor. Day after day, his calm explanation of complicated, awful news helped to reassure a traumatized city that it would pull through and that someone was in charge. He attended funerals, comforted survivors, urged residents to dine out and tourists to come in, all the while exuding compassion and resolve, even as the new threat of anthrax emerged.[3]

TO DO

- ☑ Select your team. List team members' titles and duties as well as their names.
- ☑ Designate a backup person for each team member.
- ☑ Select your library's leader-spokesperson.
- ☑ Establish a crisis chain of command. Team members will be working together closely, and knowing who's in charge will eliminate many problems when a crisis occurs.
- ☑ Create a rapid response mechanism (telephone tree, cell phone list, e-mail) for getting in touch with team members and their alternates. Practice it.
- ☑ Let everyone in the organization know who's on the team and what the lines of authority are.

#

NOTES

1. Ginnie Cooper, while director of the Multnomah County Library, Portland, Ore. Interview, Feb. 17, 2001, Portland.
2. Lawrence K. Altman and Gina Kolata, "Story of Anthrax Outbreak a Primer on What Not to Do," *The Oregonian*, Jan. 6, 2002.
3. Don Barry, "Giuliani Starts Year as Lamb, Leaves Lion," *The Oregonian*, Dec. 31, 2001.

Identifying Library Audiences and Stakeholders

CHAPTER 4

> *There is compelling evidence that giving special, customized attention to the leaders of many different constituent groups represents a "best practice" among leading organizations.*
> —David Kirk, corporate communications consultant[1]

In this chapter you will learn to identify your library's key stakeholders and the tools to stay in two-way communication with them. You will create a grid that assigns ongoing responsibility for communicating with each stakeholder group to one or more library managers.

IDENTIFYING YOUR LIBRARY'S STAKEHOLDERS

Stakeholders are individuals or groups who have a common interest and a shared stake in an organization's success. They are sometimes called *publics*, or *constituencies*.

The importance of keeping stakeholders in the loop during a crisis cannot be overstated. "The focus of our planning and our measurement must be on the quality of the relationships we build with the critical audiences whose support and understanding our organizations need to do their work," writes David Kirk in *Public Relations Tactics*.[2]

A good crisis communications plan will specifically identify your library's stakeholders and your plan for maintaining regular communication with them. It answers these questions:

> Who are your library's key stakeholders?

What means of communication do you use to keep them informed about library issues?

How will you inform them when a crisis is looming or has happened?

How will you provide regular information updates for them during a crisis?

How will you maintain their goodwill and support during and after this time?

Your stakeholders will likely fall into a few general categories: the people you serve, those who advocate for library issues, and those who provide financial support. In addition to cardholders and patrons, your stakeholders will probably include library staff, members of your governing board or library board, officers or members of your library foundation and Friends of the Library, political allies, and community leaders. Media representatives are an important public (or conduit to the public); so are police, fire, and health care agencies, especially in an emergency. Your list might also include volunteers, vendors, other libraries, neighboring businesses, people who speak another language, or any group that might be affected by something that happens at your library.

Once you've identified your stakeholders, consider the probable role of each in a crisis. Who would come to your aid? Who wouldn't?

MAINTAINING REGULAR COMMUNICATION WITH STAKEHOLDERS

Establishing and nurturing good relationships with your library's key stakeholders *right now* are the first step in maintaining their goodwill during a crisis. Don't leave this vital step to chance; assure their support by designating specific crisis team members, library administrators, or other supporters to be ongoing communications liaisons with your stakeholder groups.

How to do this? Try to determine which communications tools work best for each group. A general rule is that the smaller the stakeholder group, the more personal your ongoing communication will need to be. Most of us value face-to-face or at least voice-to-voice communication more than we do newsletters, blanket e-mails, faxes, and other less personal means. Ideally, regular meetings offer opportunities to talk with each other. Semisocial occasions encourage news sharing.

But there is only so much time, and the number of possible stakeholders is vast. That's why newsletters, e-mail discussion groups, websites, fact sheets, news releases, and other less interactive communications tools all have a place in your plan. They help to ensure that no group is left out of the information loop.

CREATING A STAKEHOLDER COMMUNICATIONS GRID

Create a stakeholder communications plan by first looking at how you communicate with your stakeholders during ordinary times. You probably use different methods for different groups. For instance, you might stay in touch with the library board using telephone conversations, e-mails, meeting notices, and minutes of meetings. With staff, you might rely on e-mail, meetings, the intranet, and faxes. To respond to questions from reporters and editors, you could mail or fax news releases, talk by telephone, or participate in interviews. To keep library users and patrons up to date, you might place information on the library website or in newsletters, brochures, posters, or flyers.

Real communication flows two ways. A good mix of tools includes plenty of opportunities for library stakeholders to ask questions and to offer comments or criticisms. Websites should allow viewers to send e-mail to the library with a single click. Newsletters and other printed materials should include phone and fax numbers, e-mail addresses, and website addresses to encourage reader feedback. Staff members should respond promptly to comments and queries.

Which of the following communications tools or methods does your library use? List them.

Person-to-Person Communication
- telephone conversations
- interviews
- staff work group and committee meetings
- all-library staff meetings
- library board meetings
- governing board meetings
- community or town hall meetings
- annual meetings
- speeches/speakers bureau

Written Communication
- e-mail
- faxed messages
- letters
- minutes of meetings
- meeting notices

Publications and Marketing Communication
- newsletters
- calendars of events
- brochures
- flyers/posters
- fact sheets or backgrounders
- histories
- white papers/special reports
- annual reports

Media Communication
- news releases
- interviews
- letters to the editor
- editorials
- op-ed pieces (opinion articles that appear on the page opposite the editorials)

Miscellaneous Communication
- library programs (story times)
- library-sponsored events (summer reading, read-a-thons, author visits)
- participation in community events
- paid advertising
- phone trees
- direct mail pieces
- other

Online Communication
>library website
>staff intranet

Now that you've identified your various modes of communication, set up your own communications grid—as a team—for each category. See figure 4-1 for an example. You'll want to set up a similar format for groups such as the library board, library foundation, Friends of the Library, volunteers, community leaders, decision makers, and other relevant groups. List your library's stakeholders and designate a crisis team member to act as the communications liaison to each stakeholder group. Specify the methods of communication you will use with each audience and the desired frequency of communication.

EDUCATING AND NURTURING STAKEHOLDERS

Educating and nurturing key stakeholders and decision makers are not only a best practice; they also make good sense. When a crisis happens, your first con-

FIGURE 4-1 Contact Information for Library Governing Board

Library staff member assigned to this stakeholder group: _____		
Communications tools that reach this group: _____		
Name:	Work phone:	E-mail:
Title:	Cell phone:	After-hours information:
Daytime address:	Pager:	
	Fax:	
Name:	Work phone:	E-mail:
Title:	Cell phone:	After-hours information:
Daytime address:	Pager:	
	Fax:	

cern will be anyone in need of immediate assistance. Initially, you may have little time to deal with the concerns of library stakeholders. As soon as possible, however, you will want to make them aware of what's going on, what's being done, how what's happened may affect them, and what they can do to help.

TO DO

- ☑ Create a contact list for each of your library's stakeholder groups. Assign a library liaison for each group and specify the tools you will use to maintain good communication with the group.
- ☑ Establish and nurture relationships with each public. Like friendships, they need tending, and like good friendships, they can provide support during critical times.
- ☑ Be alert for other stakeholder partnership possibilities that could provide valuable third-party endorsements in the event of a crisis.

#

NOTES

1. David Kirk, "Assess the Health of Your Relationships with a Relationship Checkup," *Public Relations Tactics*, July 2001.
2. Ibid.

Assessing Your Library's Crisis Potential

CHAPTER 5

Look at the year just past and ask, what if?—Sarah Long, past president of ALA[1]

In this chapter you will identify potential crises that could affect your library.

YOUR LIBRARY'S ANNUAL CHECKUP

An annual vulnerability audit will benefit your library in many ways. It will help you identify trouble spots and face them head on. It will allow you to keep watch over issues and problems that could become major. It will help you recognize the possibility of unfavorable publicity and defuse it by communicating clear and consistent messages. It will give you time to create a file of information for each potential emergency and to construct practice crisis communications scenarios that will help library staff gain experience.

Although the size and severity of crisis situations are subject to hundreds of variables—library size, the age of the facility, and the nature of the community, for example—the principles of crisis preparedness and response remain relatively constant. They start with a realistic assessment of potentially sensitive issues: maybe your library's aging buildings are barely up to earthquake or fire codes; maybe the latest round of budget cuts translate into reduced hours and staff lay-offs; maybe your library is located in a neighborhood that has experienced a rash of armed robberies; maybe your systems have been hit by the latest computer worm or virus; maybe a bomb scare recently closed a nearby community center.

A vulnerability audit is like an annual checkup. It takes a no-nonsense look at your library's current issues so that you have a better-than-even chance of spotting an at-risk situation before it happens. Out of the hundreds of crisis possibilities, you can probably identify the few that would be most likely to happen at your library. The communications strategies you implement in these situations are the core steps for dealing with that once-in-a-lifetime disaster you hope will never happen.

One of the most important things libraries can do is take time to reflect, assess, and ask, what if? Do so at least once a year; areas of potential crisis will change from year to year and even month to month.

CONDUCTING THE VULNERABILITY CHECKUP

The vulnerability audit is a team project that starts with a candid discussion of issues that could turn into crisis situations. Hard as it is to tackle sensitive topics, your library's reputation is worth any possible discomfort.

Start by assembling the crisis team for a one-day planning session. Choose a good discussion leader and someone to take notes on a flip chart or whiteboard. If your budget allows, a trained facilitator would be invaluable.

Assessing Your Library

Use the following questions to direct the discussion, and add others that are unique to your library:

> What is your library's mission statement? How does it govern all that you do?
>
> What evidence do you have about how your community perceives you? If you have survey information, what does it tell you? What anecdotal information do you have?
>
> How is staff morale? How do library staff find out about problems that may affect them? What do library staff members do when they sense potential problems?
>
> Are the library's buildings in good repair? What equipment is vulnerable?
>
> What safety measures are in place? Are these measures well known?
>
> Is there adequate security?
>
> How carefully are budget and finance records maintained? Are you comfortable with your accounting procedures?

How stable is your funding source?

What other questions should be asked that are of concern for your library?

Examining Recent Emergencies

After you've taken a candid look at the state of your library, ask: What emergencies or crises have you experienced recently? Describe the three most serious.

What was the outcome?

How well prepared were you?

What did you learn?

What grade would you give your efforts?

From your discussion of your library's previous emergencies or crises, how would you now define a crisis?

What Mini-Crises Have You Dealt with Recently?

When 25 library directors from small to medium-sized libraries were asked in September 2001 what mini-crises they had dealt with in the past several months, they listed the following (in their order and their words):

unattended dog on library lawn bites child

after-hours security personnel using library computers to run a small business

Internet access down for most of the day

person stuck in elevator

governing board administrator who knows best way to run a library

a physically threatening patron

loss of key staff person due to illness or resignation

loss of funding for library operations

staff layoffs due to lack of funding

mentally ill patrons

difficult employees

micromanagement by governing board

materials budget that can't be spent fast enough but still having to say no to other expenditures irate nonresident wanting a free card

not enough staff diversity

no bilingual staff

homeless patrons

teens using library entrances to hang out

computer problems with few staff who can troubleshoot

lice

employee burnout

The same group provided the following answers in response to a related question: In what areas might you currently be vulnerable to criticism?

censorship; Internet issues

having to ask unattended children to leave when the library closes

budget reductions resulting in layoffs and poorer service

allowing children to check out adult materials[2]

Forecasting

Now brainstorm this question: What crises could your library face in the coming months? List all suggestions. To help you get started, here, culled from news reports and websites, is an inventory of crisis issues and situations that libraries or similar organizations have faced in recent years.

PATRON PROBLEMS

angry patrons

problem patrons

patron threats

patron violence

child safety

child molestation

accusations of child molestation

latchkey kids

homeless people

BUILDING PROBLEMS

    structural problems

    aging building problems: asbestos, dry rot, leaks, cracking, mold

    poor ventilation or "bad air"

    ADA noncompliance

    rodents or other pests

STAFF PROBLEMS

    resignation, illness, or death of key library administrator

    felony charges against an administrator, trustee, foundation member, or staff member

    administrative mismanagement

    angry employees

    fired employees

    forced layoffs

    employee strikes

    employee fraud

    substance abuse

    workplace violence

COMPUTER PROBLEMS

    filtering of public computers

    computer malfunctions

    computer crashes

    computer migrations

    hacker attacks

NATURAL DISASTERS

    earthquakes

    fire

    flood or tsunami

    hurricane, cyclone, or tornado

MAN-MADE PROBLEMS
>   fire or explosion in the library
>   fire or explosion in nearby buildings
>   vandalism
>   graffiti

FINANCIAL PROBLEMS
>   faulty budget practices
>   budget shortfalls
>   budget overruns
>   embezzlement

MEDIA PROBLEMS
>   media scrutiny
>   aggressive news reporters
>   unprofessional news reporters

MISCELLANEOUS PROBLEMS
>   special interest groups
>   accusations of sexual harassment
>   accusations of racial harassment
>   materials preservation
>   lawsuits
>   food-related illness
>   rumors
>   acts of terrorism[3]

Organizing the Results

After you've brainstormed your list, group the possible emergencies and crises into categories like those outlined in the following paragraphs. In a future step, your team will practice for a real crisis by working through a scenario in each category.

MEGA-CRISES

Mega-crises shut down library service. Some examples are bombing, earthquake, flood, tornado, heat wave, fire, terrorist sabotage, major explosion, and hazardous materials spill.

VERY SERIOUS CRISES

Very serious crises affect your library's ability to provide service. Some examples are a fire that destroys the building, an aging and potentially unsafe building, an incident of workplace violence, a major power outage, a labor strike, and damage to the computer system.

SERIOUS CRISES

Some crises can have grave impact on library patrons. Examples are lawsuits, accounting errors or misdeeds, burglary, budget cutbacks, staff layoffs, sexual harassment, employee misconduct, a library board member whose business activities have come under investigation, vandalism, employee theft, and some censorship issues.

EVERYDAY EMERGENCIES

Everyday emergencies have the potential to become more serious: computer malfunctions, a lost child, Internet issues, problem patrons, graffiti, homeless people loitering on the library steps, latchkey kids, handicapped accessibility issues, human error. Someone else's disaster could also affect your library—bomb threats to neighboring buildings or businesses, for instance.

Talking through Possible Crises

Choose a crisis from each category; when possible, choose one that you've identified for your library. Talk the crisis through as a group or assign different situations to groups of two or three. Ask:

> If this crisis occurred, what warning signs might you have seen?
> If this crisis occurred, who would be the victims?
> If this crisis occurred, do you have a system in place to deal with it?
> What additional crises in this category should your library be prepared for?

Learning from Other Organizations

Researching the experience of others is a key component of the planning process. Libraries are good at this. We learn from each other through professional organizations, at conferences and workshops, in library publications, on websites, in e-mail, and in one-on-one phone conversations.

It's also important for libraries to research and learn from the experience of other types of organizations. So the next step might be take-home assignments for team members to complete before a follow-up meeting. Start the follow-up meeting by asking: What can we learn from the experience of other libraries and other organizations?

RESEARCHING OTHER LIBRARIES

Read recent library publications, check out websites, and call colleagues in other parts of the United States. Look for answers to questions like these:

> What are national library leaders saying about the possibility of potential crises?
>
> What emergencies or crises have other libraries been experiencing?
>
> What did they do right? What would they do differently next time?
>
> Did the library come off as aloof or compassionate?
>
> Did the news media perceive the library as open and helpful?
>
> How did the library communicate during the first critical hours of the crisis?
>
> How visible was the director or other library authority?

RESEARCHING OTHER ORGANIZATIONS

Use the same techniques to gather information from other public organizations. Look for answers to questions like these:

> What emergencies have other community organizations been experiencing?
>
> What did they do right?
>
> What would they do differently next time?

TO DO

With the crisis communications team, brainstorm:

- ✓ What are the three greatest threats your library faces right now?
- ✓ What three crises are you best prepared for?
- ✓ Are the crises you face and the crises you are best prepared for the same?

☑ What actions would the library need to take if one of these crises occurred?

#

NOTES

1. Sarah Long, past president, American Library Association, and director, North Suburban Library System, Chicago, Ill., when asked how an organization should begin its annual crisis appraisal. Interview, July 17, 2001, San Francisco, Calif.
2. Oregon Library Director's Fall Conference, Portland, Ore., Sept. 14, 2001.
3. An extensive index of potential crises can be found in James E. Lukaszewski, *Crisis Communication Planning Strategies: A Crisis Communication Management Workbook* (New York: Public Relations Society of America and Lukaszewski Group, 2000), 5.5–5.9. This is one in a series of books in Lukaszewski's Executive Action Crisis Communication Management System.

Creating Ready Responses for Areas of Vulnerability

CHAPTER 6

Be prepared.—Boy Scout motto

In this chapter you will analyze several emergency and crisis scenarios; then you will use this experience to create talking points for each of your library's areas of vulnerability.

You know how much easier it is to explain something when you've said it many times before? When you've discovered which points or arguments really get through to each of your audiences? The words you are using have become more persuasive because the message they convey has become clear in your own mind. These well-articulated messages have become your talking points.

Talking points are not speeches. They are nuggets of key ideas that have been thought through and put into easy-to-understand language. They can be tailored to fit any opportunity for communication that you might encounter, from a structured speech for a local Kiwanis Club to an interview with an investigative reporter to a casual conversation at the supermarket checkout counter. Thanks to your planning, practice, and familiarity with the talking points, your words flow more naturally and persuasively.

STAY AHEAD OF YOUR CRITICS: PREPARE AND PRACTICE

Consider each of the potential vulnerabilities you identified in the last chapter. As a team, identify the most difficult questions you could be asked about them.

Then gather into smaller groups to divide up the questions and prepare matter-of-fact, succinct answers that tell others why you've made the decisions you have. Share and agree upon your collective responses. These will be your talking points, the brief explanations that capture the core of the messages you wish to convey. They should be factual and straightforward. You know there are good reasons for doing the things you do; communicate that.

Practice your talking points with each other. Get comfortable working them into your conversations. Make the words part of you. Your goal is to educate and persuade, so be willing to patiently say much the same thing again and again. Remember the educator's mantra: repetition with variation. This exercise is especially important for the library's primary spokesperson, but everyone on the team should be practiced in articulating the library's key messages. Later, your library might wish to offer similar small-group training for all library staff.

Following is an example of how to respond effectively to the issue of workplace violence.

CRISIS RESPONSE EXAMPLE: WORKPLACE VIOLENCE

The Situation

According to a national survey conducted in 2001, one full-time worker out of four is harassed, threatened, or attacked on the job in the course of a year.[1] Faced with these troubling statistics, your library has identified workplace violence as a vulnerability issue and has put several new security measures into place, including new lighting, security cameras, and identification badges. You are also considering nighttime security guards.

Anticipating the Hard Questions

First, brainstorm with the team to identify questions that might arise around the library's decision to increase its security measures. For example, if the library is taking preventive security measures due to perceived threats, staff members will want to know why. What threats? What security measures? Is this still a safe place to work? Library patrons, the public, and the media will ask: Have there been dangerous incidents? Is there a pattern? Have police been involved? Have patrons or staff been at risk? What's being done to make sure everyone is safe?

Once you've identified the questions, work with the team to develop talking points. These points will not only be the basis of the library's public communication when implementing preventive security measures, but they can also be invaluable later—if a crisis is threatened or if one actually occurs.

WHEN PREVENTIVE MEASURES ARE BEING TAKEN

Because your library has identified workplace violence as a potential threat, the library is taking proactive, preventive steps. Staff members and patrons may have questions about these activities. What's going on, they may wonder. Isn't the library safe? Here's how you might address these questions:

> The safety of our staff and of our patrons is the library's highest priority *(statement of concern)*. We have all read news accounts of workplace violence. Even though our library has not experienced such violence, and even though there is little indication that such an incident would happen here, we do not take the recent threat lightly *(the facts)*. The best way to set our minds at ease is to know what we would do if such a situation did happen here. That's why library administrators are working out plans to enhance the security of our library and make it easy for us to communicate with local police, emergency authorities, and each other when the need arises *(what we are doing)*.

For staff members, you may need to add a few more points:

> You'll hear more about the plans—and have a chance to ask questions—at upcoming staff meetings *(what we are doing; we will keep you informed)*. We should not rush to fear an incident that will probably never happen, but the library will take all necessary steps to ensure your safety and the safety of our patrons *(reemphasis: statement of concern)*.

WHEN A CRISIS IS THREATENED

The talking points you drafted when implementing security measures may also be adapted if a near-crisis occurs in the library. For example, say you had to fire an employee with a spotty attendance record and a history of increasingly hostile confrontations with library staff and patrons. As he leaves the building, he threatens to come back and "get even." Staff people know this person is unstable.

Here is the crisis statement you'd issue to library staff. Note how the talking points come into play again:

> Your safety and the safety of our patrons is the library's highest priority. I reiterate this because I know that you are feeling apprehensive about rumors you may have heard about a former library employee's statements as he left our employ. We do not take such statements lightly. We have notified the police, and your supervisors will be holding staff meetings today to alert you to the security measures they have suggested. We should not rush to fear an incident that will probably never happen, but we will take all necessary steps to ensure your safety and the safety of our patrons.

WHEN "WHAT IF" OCCURS

A thirty-something patron pulls a gun out of his backpack in the crowded main room of your library and threatens to fire a shot into the ceiling. He says he has followed his ex-wife to the library and he wants to know where she is. Two quick-thinking staff members get patrons out of the way; another quietly calls the police. The patron with the gun runs out a side door and is later apprehended by law enforcement officers. No one is hurt, but the incident has justifiably triggered a spate of "Is Your Library Safe?" media stories. The public and the library staff shudder at the thought of what could have happened.

Here's your statement to the media, adapted from your talking points:

> The safety of our patrons and of our staff is the highest priority we have in the library. We are saddened that this incident happened in our library, but deeply proud of the professionalism shown by our library staff, whose first instinct was to protect our library's patrons *(statement of concern)*. We do not take this incident lightly.
>
> Even before it happened, we had instituted a plan to increase the security of our patrons and our staff. The plan includes gradual installation—as the budget permits—of new lighting, security cameras, and ID badges for library workers. These and other measures, not described here for security reasons, will make it easier for us to communicate with local police and other authorities *(the facts; what we are doing)*.
>
> We are taking and will continue to take all necessary steps—both outwardly visible and behind the scenes—to ensure the safety of our patrons and our staff. We'll continue to provide information on this very important issue. Please check our website for the latest information or call us at 123-456-7890.

Sample News Release

MIDVALE LIBRARY
123 Main St.
City, State, Zip Code
Sept. 10, 2003

For Immediate Release
Contact: Janice Smith,
Library Director, 000-234-5678
David Jones,
Maintenance Supervisor, 000-234-4567

LIBRARY STAFF REACTS QUICKLY TO SAFEGUARD PATRONS

Midvale, Ohio—Midvale Library staffers moved quickly to protect library patrons today when a distraught man entered the library's main reading room and threatened to fire a shot into the ceiling if he didn't immediately find his ex-wife. The man ran out a side door as library staff hurriedly guided patrons away and called the police. He was later apprehended and is currently being held at the Midvale County Correctional Center. No gun was found, say law enforcement officials.

"The safety of our patrons and of our staff is the library's highest priority," said Library Director Janice Smith, whose office is a few feet from the reading room. "Library staff reacted instinctively to protect our patrons, and I am very proud of their professionalism."

The incident is not being taken lightly, Smith said. Even before it happened, library officials had instituted a plan to increase the security of library users and staff. The plan includes gradual installation—as the budget permits—of new lighting, security cameras, and ID badges for library workers.

"These and other measures, some visible and some out of sight of the public, will help us ensure the safety of our patrons and our staff," Smith said.

Midvale Library will host a public meeting on Thursday, Oct. 10, to discuss safety issues at the library and in the Midvale community. The meeting will be held at 7 p.m. in the library meeting room. The library is located at 123 Main St.

###

IDEAS FOR TALKING POINTS

Working through practice crisis scenarios will help your team construct effective vulnerability responses for your library and respond more quickly and compassionately during real emergencies. Together with your team, look for news stories from newspapers, television, or websites that have to do with a crisis situation; use them as a springboard for discussion.

For example, how would you respond if any of the following incidents, all taken from actual news stories, occurred at your library?

> "Workers continue to clean up after a four-alarm fire destroyed a vacant warehouse and an adjacent building. The structure was declared a total loss."[2]
>
> "29 people suffered minor injuries when a tree fell at Disneyland on Friday, a park spokesman said. Five of the injured were taken to hospitals."[3]
>
> "Poll says public sympathy is behind striking nurses."[4]
>
> "Web worm effects continue to be felt around country."[5]

Or work through scenarios that are especially pertinent to libraries. For example, discuss and practice how your library would respond in one of the following scenarios:

> Your library building is aging. An inspection after a recent mild earthquake showed structural damage that will eventually need major repairs, even though engineers believe there is no immediate danger to library users. However, on further inspection, engineers find that interior support systems shown in the original plans were never installed, compromising the safety of the entire building.
>
> Funding cuts mean you must close a branch library, and your board directs you to close the one that would have impact on the fewest library users. The smallest library, however, is the one most frequently used by African American patrons, who feel strongly about its actual and symbolic presence in their neighborhood.
>
> Your library board president is the chief executive officer of a large accounting firm in a nearby city. A team of investigative reporters is checking out rumors that he has been embezzling from his clients' accounts. They are requesting an interview to ask about the extent of his authority and involvement with your library's financial affairs.

- A reorganization of your library's management structure has engendered much fear and anger among the staff. Your employees organize, and when negotiations break down, they threaten the first library strike in your state's history.
- One of your branch libraries was converted from an old warehouse years ago. Staff members at the building complain of headaches and congestive disorders. They are warning patrons to stay away.
- Voters have approved funds for the construction of a new library building to replace one that has become too small for a neighborhood that has grown into a densely populated community. The next step is to designate a building site, but no open site is available, so existing buildings will have to be demolished. In addition to the strong attachment citizens often feel for the buildings in their community, many are still angry about the placement of a new recreation center at a site perceived to be too far from the community center.
- Rain is falling hard, snow is melting fast, and rivers in your town are rising above flood stage. By the time the waters have crested and receded, your library system's main computer system, located in the basement of your library, has sustained extensive damage.
- A group of teenagers has taken over the sidewalk and steps of your downtown library building. The library's door count is going down, partly because many patrons are afraid of having to "run the gauntlet" of young people they perceive as oddly dressed and intimidating.
- It's your worst nightmare. A six-year-old boy has been molested in the men's restroom of your library. The distraught mother, who thought the library was a safe place, is threatening to sue the library, the library board, and anyone else she thinks might possibly be at fault.

As you work through these scenarios, ask:

What is the vulnerability issue that preceded this emergency?

What hard questions are reporters (and the public) asking?

What actions should we take?

What messages do we need to communicate?

KEY MESSAGES

Look again at the responses in the previous examples. Note the three key messages that are essential in any crisis situation. They are:

> The library's first *concern* is for the welfare of those who are hurt or affected in any way.
>
> These are the *facts* as we know them now.
>
> We will *keep you informed* as we get new information.

TO DO

Now it's your turn to draft your library's crisis responses.

- ☑ Prepare a worksheet similar to the one in figure 6-1 to aid you and your team in organizing your thoughts. Make as many copies as you need—one for each of the sensitive issues you've identified for your library.

- ☑ With the crisis team, use the worksheet to draft brief talking points for each area of vulnerability and potential crisis that you identified in the previous chapter. Be sure to include the key messages mentioned earlier. Ask: Why is this a sensitive area for our library? Who are the key audiences we need to communicate with about this issue? What result do we want?

- ☑ As you work, create files on your library's vulnerable areas. Include magazine articles, speeches, position papers, news coverage, and statements from third-party experts who can speak to the library's position.

- ☑ If you have especially volatile issues, consider writing draft news releases as well. See appendixes 1 and 2 for suggestions and a sample release.

FIGURE 6-1 Talking Points

Area of Vulnerability _____
Issue:
Tough questions to be prepared for:
Response (underline the three key messages):

#

NOTES

1. Tamara Jones, "Terror on the Job," *Good Housekeeping*, January 2001.
2. "Still Picking Up after Fire," *The Oregonian*, Jan. 31, 2001.
3. "Twenty-nine People Suffer Injuries As Tree Topples at Disneyland," *The Oregonian*, May 5, 2001.
4. Joe Rojas-Burke, "Poll Says Public Sympathy Is behind Striking Nurses, *The Oregonian*, Jan. 31, 2002.
5. "Web Worm Effects Continue to Be Felt around Country," *The Oregonian*, Jan. 28, 2003.

Building Positive Media Relationships

CHAPTER 7

> *Media coverage goes to those firms that have taken the time to cultivate lasting relationships with the media based on mutual trust and respect.*
> —Margo M. Mateas, public relations training company[1]

In this chapter you will learn strategies for creating good relationships with reporters and editors before a crisis occurs and practical ideas for working with them during a crisis. You will add these strategies to your communications kit along with key media contact information.

WORKING WITH THE MEDIA BEFORE A CRISIS OCCURS

Start now to establish a solid working relationship with reporters and editors. During a time of crisis, your library's awareness of the media and record of cooperation with the working press will be a crucial factor in how the media portrays you and how the public perceives you.

Reporters and editors perform a valuable service that libraries need: they convey information to their readers and listeners. If it seems like the media hold more cards in the library-media relationship, it helps to remember that professional journalists and professional librarians have much in common: both share a passion for knowledge and the freedom of information guaranteed by the First Amendment.

So how do you build rapport with reporters and editors and earn their respect before a crisis occurs? You do it by taking every opportunity to provide them with accurate, timely information; by being readily accessible when they call; and by consistently providing them with the same good information service libraries strive to give all patrons.

Nothing helps a library's reputation more than becoming known as *the* place where a reporter can get an answer, even if the answer is "I don't know, but I'll do my best to find out for you," or "There's nothing new yet, but I'll let you know as soon as we find out more." Reporters will inevitably call with questions at times when you just can't squeeze another task into an impossibly busy day. But providing information is what we do, and these are golden opportunities to enhance your library's reputation.

Give reporters your library's telephone information number, inviting them to call when they need to check a fact or find an authority in a particular subject. Post phone numbers for key library staff on your website. Rotate "person-in-charge" assignments so that someone knowledgeable about the library is always available when reporters call, even after hours. Once you've provided information for them when they're in a time crunch, they'll be back.

Knowledgeable library staff can be called upon to help. Offer them basic media training to increase their comfort level with the media. They should understand the role of the media in society and the community, how the media works, how a reporter's job differs from an editor's, who writes headlines, and what's on or off the record. If the training budget is tight, tap into the (pro bono) community spirit of local reporters or communications experts by inviting them to the library to meet informally with library managers and staff.

When media folks call, give their needs the highest priority. They will inevitably be on a deadline, so make sure all staff members know they should immediately route media calls to the director or the public relations office.

Build and Nurture Your Media Relationships

Read, listen to, watch, and log on to local, regional, and national media. Read your local daily newspaper religiously; it often sets the news agenda for the other media in your community. Stay tuned in to the issues your community is talking about. Pay special attention to reporter bylines, editorials, op-ed pieces, and letters to the editor. Include members of editorial boards on your media contact list; their opinions and their words have power to influence others, especially during controversies. Educate them about what libraries do.

If you haven't already done so, set up a system of planned communication with regular news releases, phone conversations, interviews, fact sheets, backgrounders, and other informational tools. Your goal is to provide reporters and editors with ongoing, newsworthy items about your library. When an emergency or crisis occurs, they will already know your library. Refer to the list of your library's in-place communication tools that you compiled in chapter 2 (figure 2-3).

Be realistic about what's news, and understand that you do not control what's printed or aired. The only way you can be sure your message will appear exactly as you want it is with paid advertising. Think like a journalist; avoid fluff masquerading as news. Ask media folks how they define what's news. Find out how and when they like to receive news items. Avoid harassing busy editors with follow-up phone calls or long voice mails.

Be aware of media deadlines. Daily newspapers may have a general deadline, but with instant website updating and several overnight editions, they can quickly adapt to include breaking news. Given a choice, television reporters prefer to gather news in the morning so they have time to prepare it for the 5 p.m. news shows. Radio has immediacy; you can do a live radio interview by telephone at 11:30 a.m. and hear the segment repeated on the noon newscast. Weekly news outlets are usually very busy the day before publication.

Take Time to Educate Reporters

Busy reporters often have little or no knowledge of the library or library issues. Talking basics with them pays off. So does providing written information that they can take away with them—brochures, fact sheets, backgrounders, news releases, issues statements, copies of speeches. Invite them to check your website for up-to-date information, and be available for follow-up questions as they write their stories.

New reporters need special attention. Generally, the smaller the media organization (weekly or monthly newspapers, small radio stations, newsletter groups), the less experienced their reporters will be and the more likely they'll be to misinterpret or misuse information. Be patient. Take the time to educate them by inviting them for an interview and a tour. When they leave, send a press kit with them.

Update reporter contact information regularly. News reporters change beats and jobs. It's important to create a good media contact list, and it's just as important to maintain it well, using a format similar to that shown in figure 7-1. If your library is small, assign this task to a volunteer or intern.

Be sure your website is reporter-friendly. Reporters will not use information from your website unless they trust its accuracy and timeliness. A vital part of

FIGURE 7-1 Contact Information for Local Media (Newspapers, TV, Radio)

| Library staff member assigned to this stakeholder group: _____ |||
Communications tools that reach this group: _____		
Name:	Work phone:	E-mail:
Title:	Cell phone:	After-hours information:
Daytime address:	Pager:	
	Fax:	
Name:	Work phone:	E-mail:
Title:	Cell phone:	After-hours information:
Daytime address:	Pager:	
	Fax:	

investing in a website is investing in the human resources necessary to manage it and keep it up to date. That means daily, sometimes hourly. Reporters on deadline will be able to find information on your website more easily if there is a linked site to a media center or press room. Include contact information for library administrators, a news release archive, backgrounders, fact sheets, and other materials.

Internet chat sites and talk radio are worth monitoring; reporters read and listen to these, too. If a library issue comes up, you might wish to join in the conversation by offering the library's position; or you might decide that responding will give an issue more attention than it deserves. In any case, be ready for media calls.

WORKING WITH THE MEDIA DURING A CRISIS

Even though your library's goal is to prevent a crisis, an emergency is an opportunity to demonstrate what libraries do well: gather fast, accurate information.

Reporters can be a big help in getting information out during an emergency. This is where the long-term relationships with the press and your reputation for honesty pay off. There is never a guarantee that the coverage will be entirely positive, but without your history of cooperation, it could be worse. A good relationship will also hasten the return to normal press coverage.

During a crisis, reporters will want information quickly, probably more quickly than you are able to gather it. Broadcast news reporters will want the basics immediately: who, what, where, when, and why. Print news reporters will have more time and more questions, but their website editors will want to publish information as quickly as they can get it. Newspapers usually go with a straight news story the first day and then follow up on succeeding days with more detail.

Position the Library as a Key Source of Information

Get comfortable with knowing that you can influence media coverage, but you can't control it. That said, maintain as much control as possible by making sure the library is a major source of the information that is being disseminated.

Today, information moves with Internet speed, and you have to stay ahead of it in a crisis. Dig out the facts as quickly as possible so that you can respond at once to media inquiries. Explain what you are doing about the problem and who is involved in finding a solution. Speak frequently to the press and the public about what you know, even if you must say there is nothing new. Assure them that you will update everyone as soon as more facts become available.

When you do have information to share, make sure it is accurate and verifiable. Never lie or cover up. If the news is bad, it's better that the public hear it from you. By presenting the news, you frame the debate. The basic rule of information gathering is the same for journalists as it is for libraries: get it fast and get it right.

HOW TO TALK TO THE PRESS

When facing the press in a crisis, keep these caveats in mind:

- ✓ Don't speak off the record. Assume everything you say is for publication.
- ✓ Don't say "No comment." Say "This is what we know at this time."
- ✓ Don't speak in absolutes. Allow yourself some breathing room, especially if all the facts are not in.
- ✓ Don't be afraid to say, "I don't know." Say what we say every day to patrons: "I'll find out and get back to you."
- ✓ Don't speculate about why something happened.
- ✓ Don't talk about damage estimates, especially in terms of money.
- ✓ Don't allocate blame.
- ✓ Anticipate possible hostility, and don't take it personally. Your practice in talking about vulnerability issues will pay off.
- ✓ Think visually. How will this look on the five o'clock news or on a website?

The reporters covering you during an emergency may not be the ones who cover you day to day, so provide them and their editors with press kits that contain news releases, a statement from the director, library background information, and other pertinent information. Make sure these materials are easily available on your website (see figure 2-4) and link them to the crisis information site as well. Add new information as it becomes available.

Be proactive in keeping the library's talking points in front of the press and the public. Don't allow much time to elapse between statements, even if you say the same thing. A steady stream of information reinforces the perception that someone is doing something. If reporters don't request an interview, you might contact them, saying, "I thought you would want to know about . . ." or "I know you have been covering this situation and I'd be happy to provide you with more information. Can we schedule an interview?" You might also arrange tours for reporters; these become opportunities for photos and informal interviews.

Misinformation is hard to retract. If false information gets out, be proactive. If a reporter gets something wrong, consider whether the error is important enough to warrant the time to correct it. If it is, call the reporter to clarify the facts. Then fax the corrected information to the reporter and to the library's stakeholders. Take care not to refer to the error by repeating it in the text of the clarification. If possible, assign someone to monitor web rumors and misinformation during a crisis.

Be Ready for Interviews

Keep these suggestions in mind when you are being interviewed:

- ✓ Know what you want your message to be. Don't always wait for questions—create opportunities to reinforce your message.
- ✓ Use your vulnerability issues model to identify the tough questions.
- ✓ Practice brief, nondefensive responses.
- ✓ Have the latest information at your fingertips.
- ✓ Don't use acronyms and library jargon. Use short sentences.
- ✓ Keep your cool when the questions are hostile. Stay positive and remember the confidence you've gained by practicing your talking points.
- ✓ If the interview is for television, choose a setting that is synonymous with the library—out in front, perhaps, or in the book stacks. Try to have the name of your library in the background.
- ✓ If the interview is for print, find out if a photographer will be coming.

Think Twice about Scheduling a News Conference

A news conference must have enough interest to draw reporters because they generally do not like receiving news that they perceive as "canned," especially when colleagues from competing media are present. Plan one only if you truly have news to impart or you are bombarded with phone calls asking the same questions and you have no other way to handle them all.

If you do schedule a news conference, identify the library's main talking points and practice answering the difficult or hostile questions you might receive in a free-for-all interview. If possible, stage a dress rehearsal. For maximum credibility, feature key decision makers, including elected or appointed authorities, the library director, and board chairperson at the news conference. Set the tone by delivering a short opening statement that describes the situation and the latest information. Prepare handouts and post them on the website afterward.

Caveat: News conferences are usually just as time-consuming as interviews. One-on-one meetings are almost always preferable, both for the library and for the reporter. You'll get better coverage if you tailor your discussion to a specific medium.

TO DO

- ☑ Create a contact list of local and regional media relevant to your library; add it to your communications kit. Using a worksheet like the one shown in figure 7-1, assign library staff or volunteers to gather names, phone numbers, cell phone numbers, pager numbers, and e-mail addresses of local and regional news reporters, editors, editorial board members, columnists, and media support staff. Include after-hours phone numbers when possible. This may very well be the most important list you'll carry with you in your crisis communications kit.

- ☑ Use a worksheet like the one in figure 7-2 to create another list that includes names, phone numbers, cell phone numbers, and e-mail addresses of national library media: reporters, editors, columnists, and support staff.

- ☑ Assign responsibility for keeping the media lists up to date and for making sure all managers and crisis communications team members carry the latest information.

- ☑ See appendixes 1 and 2 for tips on writing news releases and a sample crisis-related release.

- ✓ Schedule media training for library staff and others who need to know how to work with reporters and editors. Consider asking a panel of reporters to volunteer their time and advice.
- ✓ Make fostering an attitude of cooperation with the media a priority goal for your library.
- ✓ Take steps now to position your library as *the* place to go when media representatives and their readers or viewers need information.

FIGURE 7-2 Contact Information for Library Media

Library staff member assigned to this stakeholder group: _____		
Communications tools that reach this group: _____		
Name:	Work phone:	E-mail:
Title:	Cell phone:	After-hours information:
Daytime address:	Pager:	
	Fax:	
Name:	Work phone:	E-mail:
Title:	Cell phone:	After-hours information:
Daytime address:	Pager:	
	Fax:	

#

NOTE

1. Margo M. Mateas, "The Profiler," *Public Relations Strategist,* Fall 2001.

Communicating during a Crisis

CHAPTER 8

Emotions and feelings give significance and meaning to information. They serve as important signals of what's important and significant.
—Jennifer George, professor, Rice University[1]

In this chapter you will learn the importance of speaking out quickly and compassionately. You will add step-by-step crisis communication guides to your communications kit.

THE POWER OF EMOTION: MESSAGES WITH FEELING

"Our hearts go out to the victims and their families. We will do everything we possibly can to help at this sad time." Words like these may sometimes seem overused or hackneyed, but when delivered with heartfelt compassion, they are reassuring in a time of crisis.

When reporters asked New York Mayor Rudy Giuliani how many people were dead after the collapse of the World Trade towers, Giuliani didn't get caught up in numbers and statistics. He understood that during a time of incredibly high emotion, he needed to respond with sensitivity. More objective words would come later.

Giuliani's humane yet take-charge leadership during the World Trade Center disaster earned him the nation's ongoing praise. In a broadcast a few weeks later, ABC news anchor Peter Jennings advised the nation's leaders to follow Giuliani's example. Talk from the heart, Jennings said, "like a father or a brother." Instead of frightening people, be genuine. We will accept scary news from people we trust.[2]

Emphasize the Library's First Concern: Anyone Who Is Hurt or in Danger

When the world as we know it takes an unexpected turn, we want to know that someone is in charge. Speaking out quickly and from the heart has a calming effect. Someone is doing something.

The library's concern for anyone who may be hurt or in jeopardy is a message we can communicate at once, even before all the details of a crisis are known. While expressing our concern, this type of "holding" statement may buy some time to gather information. The statement should be brief and immediate. An example:

> We're aware of the situation and will do everything we can to help. Our hearts go out to the victims and their families. We are gathering information as quickly as possible and will keep you up to date as it becomes available.
>
> The library is a responsible community leader. Our number one concern is the welfare and safety of everyone involved in this crisis. We are acting in a way that is consistent with our mission, which is to serve our community, and we will continue to do so during this difficult time.

WHAT TO DO IMMEDIATELY

The first few minutes and hours of a crisis are critical. This is when information will be framed in the public's mind—information that will be hard to turn around later. Having a team in place to gather facts and provide a rapid response helps your organization's credibility. Doing the opposite—not speaking or speaking too late—encourages public distrust.

Following are practical suggestions for what to do in the immediate aftermath of a crisis.

Gather Information

What happened? Where did it happen? Who was affected? Why did it happen? What's being done? When will more information be available? Information gathering is what libraries do well; use those fact-finding skills now to answer these and other pressing questions. As part of your research, use your vulnerability assessment to help you identify tough questions you will be asked. Even if the crisis at hand is not one you've specifically prepared for, one of your scenarios can probably be adapted to the situation.

 Develop a Strategy

No one person can do all that needs to be done, so assemble the crisis communications team at once to divide up responsibilities. Review the methods you will use to keep each other and key stakeholders informed. Decide if there is a need for additional communications staff. If so, look for professional communicators as volunteers.

 Prepare and Disseminate a Statement

Write a statement that anticipates the tough questions you are likely to get. Explain what happened and what you are doing about the situation. Say only what you know, and speak in general terms until more solid information is available. Stress ways in which the library is acting in the best interests of its patrons and other affected groups. You don't have to memorize the statement, but get comfortable with it so you can work the messages into conversation when questions or opportunities arise.

Deliver the statement to the media and take questions. This is the responsibility of the leader-spokesperson. The director, board chair, or other library leader has more credibility with the public than an anonymous library spokesperson. Make sure that anyone who speaks to the media has these key messages in written form.

 Enlist the Help of the Media

Focus reporters and editors on delivering emergency information that will help people. You can assist by providing hard copies of your message statement and by making the library director, board chair, or other authority easily accessible for comments (reiterations of the message statement). Distribute the statement to your media contact lists by fax and e-mail and post it to your website immediately.

Members of the press will want to know:

- the basic facts as they are known at the moment
- what the library is doing in response to the emergency
- when more information will be available
- where more information can be found

✓ Distribute Key Messages to All Staff; Speak with One Voice

Stay in touch with library staff using the intranet, fax, phone, or e-mail system that you've already set up as part of your crisis communications plan. Staff will need ongoing information to answer questions from patrons, friends, and the community. Assign a crisis communications team member to keep staff up to date. The most important message to staff: "Your help is essential. We are in this together and you are needed to make our real job—providing good library service—keep happening. When this is over, we want our good reputation to remain intact."

Reemphasize the need for the library to speak with one voice, and remind staff that there is a clear chain of command during an emergency. Media requests and requests for information beyond the scope of the basic talking points need to be referred to the crisis center headquarters.

✓ Distribute Key Messages to Stakeholders

Follow through with each audience of stakeholders. Each constituency needs to be kept up to date by the team member or library manager assigned to that group. Activate the message delivery system that you set up in your crisis communications plan, the one that links designated crisis team members or library managers with specific stakeholders. Follow the plan to assure that the information team members relay is consistent with the talking points.

✓ Go to the Crisis Site

Don't be tempted to hide out. It is important for key people to be visible as soon as possible as a way of demonstrating their concern and involvement. Remember the Exxon CEO, who couldn't be found after the *Valdez* oil spill? Remember Rudolph Giuliani, who rushed to Ground Zero?

WHAT TO DO AS SOON AS POSSIBLE

✓ Set Up a Crisis Center and Media Information Center

Make sure all media calls are routed to the information center. This is a crucial step; the public will want information, and if they don't get it from the library they will find it elsewhere. The library will have more control over information flow if the information comes from the library first. Designate library staff to stay in touch with stakeholder groups, answer questions, and quell rumors; if necessary, call in local communications professionals—identified in your crisis communications planning—to help.

Continue to work from the same script. Use the earlier statement to write a news release that indicates what is known at this point in time. Present any new facts and include a quote from the director or other library official. Continue to convey compassion and concern. Distribute the release quickly, using the media contact list you maintain as part of your crisis communications plan. Also assemble press kits that contain library backgrounders, fact sheets, a director profile, photos, and other materials that may be relevant.

✓ Activate the Library's Crisis Information Website

Your website will become your online crisis communications center—*the* information tool that keeps media, patrons, and other stakeholders informed throughout the crisis. Assign responsibility for keeping the website current. Think of it as the front page of the daily newspaper or the lead stories on the five o'clock news. If your crisis communications plan is in place, your crisis communications web page already exists, ready to link to or replace your site's front page.

✓ Begin a Media Log

Keep track of all media calls and coverage using a log like the one shown in figure 8-1. The information will help identify reporters/editors and their interests and make sure each is called back. It will also be invaluable data for evaluation when the crisis is over.

✓ Create New Channels of Communication

Set up ways for the public to ask questions via your website, a telephone hotline, or e-mail. Develop a list of frequently asked questions with brief answers and distribute it to staff, your website, and relevant stakeholders. For internal communications, set up a staff hotline or intranet. Schedule regular staff meetings to share information and concerns.

✓ Give People Something to Do

Whether it's moving library materials out of a flood's way, bringing food, providing rides home for stranded people, or organizing a candlelight vigil, find ways to involve those who want to help. When bad things happen, helping others helps control our own feelings of panic. And it's often what we remember after the crisis is over.

FIGURE 8-1   Media Log

Reporter:	Date/time:	Question:	Who responded?
Work phone:			
Media organization:			
Reporter:	Date/time:	Question:	Who responded?
Work phone:			
Media organization:			

Speak Out Often

"In a country that craves information, it's better to give too much information than not enough," Office of Homeland Security Director Tom Ridge said about the anthrax scare.[3] During an emergency, key messages and talking points need to be repeated consistently and often; once is not enough. People first need to *hear* a message; then they need time to *process* it before they can *understand* it. Advertising professionals know that frequency is as important as the message itself. Say it often; say it in different ways; say it in different contexts. Say it in an initial statement to the press; put it on your website; and mention it in interviews, news releases, memos, and reports.

HOW TO COMBAT NEGATIVE PUBLICITY

- ✓ Stay visible and available; continue to show compassion.
- ✓ Perform an act of goodwill. Set up crisis phone lines, coordinate blood donations, or create an electronic crisis information center on the library's website.
- ✓ Encourage library support groups to speak out on your behalf. Third-party messages have added credibility, and others can say good things about you that you can't say for yourself.
- ✓ If negative activist groups spring up, meet with them to provide information and to combat rumors.
- ✓ Avoid using inflammatory language. You'll look guilty if you respond defensively or in anger.
- ✓ Keep the library website up to date, and include as much information as you can. Err on the side of information overload.
- ✓ Stay in touch with reporters. Repeat the key messages, especially in the context of new information. Conversations and interviews can result in favorable coverage later on.
- ✓ Pay attention to how you are being perceived. Remember that you are managing for the long term. When the crisis is over, the library's actions will remain in the public mind.
- ✓ Consider including training in dealing with confrontation in your crisis communications plan.

TO DO

- ☑ Post breaking information to the website as quickly as possible. Update often.
- ☑ Create quick links to sites that provide aid (e.g., Centers for Disease Control).
- ☑ Check all background information on website to make sure it's current.
- ☑ Refer your stakeholders to the website for the latest information.

#

NOTES

1. Jennifer George, professor of management and psychology, Rice University, as quoted by Kelli B. Newman in "The Power of Emotion," *Public Relations Tactics*, July 2001.
2. Peter Jennings, "Communicating during a Crisis," *ABC Evening News*, Oct. 24, 2001.
3. Sandra Sobieraj, "Crisis Officials Offer Public Reassurance," *The Oregonian*, Oct. 19, 2001.

After the Crisis: A Time of Opportunity

CHAPTER 9

When the crisis is over, what people hear, believe, and remember is what matters most. —Merrie Spaeth, crisis communications counselor[1]

In this chapter you will learn the importance of communication in bringing closure to an emergency or crisis. The goal is to reinforce the positive messages that library stakeholders and the community will remember long after the crisis is past.

WHAT PEOPLE HEAR, BELIEVE, AND REMEMBER

During a crisis, our first concern must be helping everyone involved, showing real concern and empathy, containing the situation. At the same time, however, we are mindful of how our actions are being perceived by the public.

The chances are excellent that your preparation has paid off and you've weathered the crisis. You've demonstrated responsible community leadership. You've done the best you can to show your patrons, your staff, and the public that their library and those who oversee it are worthy of their trust. You've learned more than you ever wanted to know about crisis communications. Reinforcing this perception—right now, when everyone is paying attention more than ever—is an opportunity not to be missed. It is one of the most important steps in your crisis communications plan.

AFTER THE CRISIS

The aftermath of a crisis may be bittersweet. It may be a time for healing, reflection, celebration, or all three. It's definitely a time to say thank you, to assess what you've learned, and to share what you've learned. It's a time to be humble, but also a time to be proud.

Celebrate the End of the Crisis

Create an event that fits your community and sends a signal of closure. Choose something that the event symbolizes: healing, reassurance, connectedness, a return to normal.

Some suggestions? Invite your community to an open house or a block party in front of the library. Ask the local high school marching band to play. Publicly honor the heroes. Ask a local author to write an epitaph or an elegy. Bury something that depicts the crisis: a brick, a tattered book, a photo. Create a giant thank-you card for people to sign. March en masse to city hall carrying signs that thank council members for their leadership.

Brainstorm ideas with your crisis team and library staff.

Say Thank You

Recognizing the good work of all who helped during the crisis is vital; say thank you again and again. Are there people who symbolize the crisis? If so, tell their stories: invite them to the library for a public acknowledgment. Send letters of commendation to their supervisors, and mention them in speeches. Write a letter to the editor of your local paper or take out an ad thanking the entire community for pulling together during a difficult time.

Debrief

Gather the crisis team and other stakeholder representatives. As blamelessly as possible, assess:

> Why did the crisis happen?
> What actions did the library take in response to the emergency?
> What could the participants have done differently?
> Could the crisis have been prevented?
> What might have been worse had it not been for the library's actions?
> What larger issues, if any, are involved?
> What problems still need to be addressed?
> What did we learn?
> Did we provide accurate and timely information?
> Did we show our concern for those affected by the crisis?

Did we safeguard our staff, patrons, and public?

Did we safeguard the library's reputation?

And the big question: How well did our crisis communications plan work?

Work to Restore Stakeholder Trust

"Trust is built over time, based on what companies do, not say," writes Chris Atkins, founder of the Ketchum Reputational Laboratory. "The bond of trust is forged through a variety of interactions between a company and its stakeholders."[2]

To find out if the bond of trust between your library and its stakeholders is still strong, survey each group—staff, patrons, supporters, library governors, and the media—at least informally. Use the library stakeholder grid assignments presented in chapter 4 to make sure no group is left out. Allow stakeholders to talk through the crisis and the debriefing, and use their input to pinpoint where relationships need rebuilding.

Work especially to reassure library staff. Back-to-normal observances are as important to the staff as they are to the public. Staff meetings, work-group exercises, individual counseling—all may be necessary to help everyone feel right again. This would be an excellent time to plan a staff retreat. The agenda might include role-playing crisis scenarios, a discussion of the importance of speaking with one voice, and information on the role of the media. Be sure to add something that's fun.

Strengthen Working Relationships with Media

Monitor media coverage, including chat rooms, message boards, and discussion groups. Schedule meetings with reporters and editors to talk about how the library and media representatives worked together and how you can continue to do so. Stay in touch with the reporters who covered the crisis. Chances are they know more about library issues than they did before and will want to do more library-related news stories.

Adapt, Modify, Change

Follow through on promises made to the public. Find the funds to develop communications tools—publications and web pages, for example—that tell them what you're doing. Take advantage of this teachable moment to inform library patrons and the general public of plans for the future, how problems will be solved, and what's being done to make things better. There are natural times to make organizational changes. This is one of them.

Prepare for the Next Emergency or Crisis

Avoiding a crisis is a whole lot better than managing one, so update your library's vulnerability portfolio now. Review the performance and makeup of the crisis communications team and modify as necessary. Integrate crisis communications planning into your ongoing library management.

Write a Narrative

Write a report that describes the events that occurred and how the library dealt with them. Use your media log; include news coverage, photos, and statements. Present your report at the next board of governors meeting and put it on the website. Don't forget to gather it all together as an entry for the John Cotton Dana Library Public Relations Award!

Share the Knowledge You've Gained

One of the best ways to share the knowledge you've gained from your crisis experience is to encourage and lead public discussion. Consider these suggestions:

- Offer to speak to local groups about the experience—the chamber of commerce, Kiwanis, Rotary, or PTA.
- Schedule community meetings, forums, or workshops to allow the community to talk about the incident and put it behind them.
- Encourage questions from the Friends of the Library, the library foundation, and local civic groups.
- Meet with editorial boards.
- Update your website. Include an informal survey to measure user opinion about how the library managed the crisis.
- Start planning a commemorative event to be held a year from now.

CONCLUSION: A CRISIS COMMUNICATIONS SUCCESS STORY

Maria E. Foley of Boston told the following story in a paper she wrote for a graduate degree program in communications management at Syracuse University.[3]

At 2:30 a.m. Saturday, July 17, 1999, Lt. Gary L. Jones, chief of public affairs for the United States Coast Guard District 1 office in Boston, learned that a small plane carrying John F. Kennedy Jr. and his wife and sister-in-law was late arriving at Martha's Vineyard Airport. Knowing that media interest would soon be intense, he immediately called his boss, Rear Admiral Richard Larrabee, and the rest of the public affairs team.

By the time Jones got to his office at 3:30 a.m., twenty-five reporters had already arrived. Jones and his team members spent several frenzied days gathering information, updating the website, granting phone interviews, and holding media briefings. With Larrabee as the spokesperson and with more than a thousand media representatives from around the world rushing to the site, the team worked to brief the media and the public on what was happening, what the Coast Guard was doing about it, and what would be happening next.

"We knew there was the media aspect, we knew there was the operational aspect, and we definitely wanted to respect the privacy of the families. We had to balance the needs of the family and the media and perform the search-and-rescue," Jones said later of the "triangle" approach. Families, they agreed, would receive the most up-to-date information before any media interviews or briefings.

On the second day of the crisis, Jones and the Coast Guard set up a joint information center to coordinate the communications of all the agencies involved—the Air Force, Navy, Air National Guard, Civil Air Patrol, National Transportation Safety Board, National Oceanic and Atmospheric Administration, and the Massachusetts State Police. Eventually, more than 60 people were gathering and preparing information. All fell under the overall direction of the Coast Guard.

On Tuesday, July 20, the bodies were recovered. The next day, they were buried at sea off the coast of Martha's Vineyard. But the media inquiries did not stop with the burial. For several days, the information center fielded questions about the amount of time and money spent on the search. In the end, reporters who covered the crisis gave the Coast Guard high marks for its efforts.

Lasting Impression: Positive

"The Coast Guard understood what the media needed," said Sean Hennessey, reporter for Boston's WHDH-TV. "They recognized the need for information and public interest in this story." The lasting impression of the Coast Guard in Boston's management of the tragic Kennedy plane crash was a positive one.

YOUR CRISIS PLAN: A WORK IN PROGRESS

Crisis planning takes time—time the U.S. Coast Guard and other crisis-ready organizations were willing to spend to protect their good reputations. So it is with our libraries.

Today, forward-thinking library managers know that emergencies and crises are opportunities to showcase their libraries' strengths. They understand that even though it is impossible to predict every emergency that could occur, they can identify and plan for crises. By confronting their vulnerabilities head-on, they reap significant rewards: a heightened sense of control, less fear of the unknown, a lower organizational stress level, and a big head start when crisis does occur.

In discussing her experience with crisis planning, Sarah Long, former president of the American Library Association, notes, "The best things in my life have come from painful situations. Now when nasty things walk in the door, I say, 'Come on in; let's think about this.' Not with fear, but with a confidence that lets that threatening thing come near. And I learn from it."[4]

Now is the time to create an action plan (see figure 9-1) for *your* library. The information you gathered as you finished each chapter of this book will form the backbone of your own crisis communications planning efforts.

FIGURE 9-1 Post-Crisis Actions

Action:	Goal:	Assigned to:	Timeline:
Action:	Goal:	Assigned to:	Timeline:

###

NOTES

1. Merrie Spaeth, crisis communications counselor, as quoted by Florida International professor Bill Adams, APR (Accredited by the Public Relations Society of America), in "Ask the Professor," *Public Relations Tactics*, September 1999.
2. Chris Atkins, "Restoring Trust in Business," *Public Relations Strategist*, Winter 2003.
3. Maria E. Foley, "Strategic Communications Lessons of the Kennedy Plane Crash," *Public Relations Strategist*, Fall 2000.
4. Sarah Long, past president, American Library Association, and director, North Suburban Library System, Chicago, Ill. Interview, July 17, 2001, San Francisco, Calif.

Twenty Tips for Writing an Effective News Release

APPENDIX 1

Reporters and editors receive stacks of news releases every day. You can increase the chances of your releases being read and used if you heed the following tips.

1. Become familiar with each newspaper, television station, radio station, and online medium that provides news about your organization.
2. Learn basic protocols of journalism so you can package your information to look and sound like news. (The *Associated Press Stylebook and Briefing on Media Law* will help. Be sure you have the latest edition.)
3. Understand that reporters will not use your release verbatim. Most often, they will use the information you provide in a news story that they will write. Be aware that news reporters do not write headlines; their editors do.
4. When writing your news release, ask: What do readers want to know? Is your event, for example, the largest of its kind? The first? The only? Will it change people's lives in any way? Will it mean jobs for people? Is a person with name recognition involved? Is the topic one that everyone's talking about? Then write a lead sentence or paragraph that announces the topic and frames its presentation. Try to mention benefits to the reader, viewer, or listener. Follow up with paragraphs that present the rest of the information, from most important to least important.
5. Include a brief topic headline that captures the essence of the message. Include a subject and a verb.
6. Avoid editorial comment. Keep it objective—just the facts. Don't use hyperbole or try to disguise advertising as news. If you want to add an opinion, quote someone.
7. Eliminate general, self-serving statements. Instead of saying "It was another wonderful library event and everyone had a great time," say

"Over 75 children and parents kept the local author busy answering questions for 45 minutes following her presentation."
8. Keep the release brief. Attach a fact sheet or backgrounder if you need to add more information.
9. Include the name and phone number of at least one person who can be contacted for further information. Make sure that person is prepared to speak with the media and is available for a period of time after the release is sent.
10. Write short sentences and short paragraphs.
11. Write in active voice.
12. Avoid library jargon; use everyday words. Also avoid acronyms.
13. Double-check all facts.
14. Double-check grammar and spelling. Don't rely on your computer's spell-check.
15. If your release will be mailed or faxed, double space it on library letterhead or on plain white paper. Be sure to include a date.
16. Ask reporters and editors how they would like to receive your news: by fax, e-mail, or U.S. mail?
17. Do not ask to approve a journalist's story before it's published.
18. Generally speaking, editors do not appreciate follow-up phone calls to "see if you need more information."
19. Alert media before an event. An event generally has more news value before it happens.
20. Don't rely solely on uncontrolled mass media to get your information out. Publishing your own newsletters, brochures, and websites allows you to control the library's message and manner of presentation.

Sample News Release

APPENDIX 2

MIDVALE LIBRARY
123 Main St.
City, State, Zip Code
Sept. 10, 2003

For Immediate Release
Contact: Janice Smith,
Library Director, 000-234-5678
David Jones, Maintenance Supervisor, 000-234-4567

BOILER BURSTS AT MIDVALE LIBRARY; INJURIES ARE MINOR

Midvale, Ohio—A boiler in the basement of the Midvale Library burst this morning, flooding the concrete floor with steaming hot water. Two library maintenance workers sustained minor burns. Both were treated at Midvale Community Hospital and released.

Maintenance staff were able to seal off the boiler quickly and stop the flooding, according to Library Director Janice Smith.

"We're thankful that no one was seriously hurt," Smith said. "There was some damage to library books and other materials that were stored in the basement. Repairs on the boiler have begun and we are looking into the reasons for its failure. Our records show that it was installed in 1982 and that it has received yearly maintenance checks."

The library remains open to the public. Regular hours are 10 a.m. to 8 p.m. Monday through Thursday, 10 a.m. to 6 p.m. Friday and Saturday, and noon to 5 p.m. on Sunday.

# # #

GLOSSARY

Beat. A reporter's regular assignment, as in "the city hall beat."

Byline. A line, usually located beneath the headline, that gives the name of the reporter who wrote the news story.

Controlled media. Media over which an organization exercises control in terms of content and presentation, as in organizational newsletters, brochures, or paid advertising.

Cutline. The caption beneath a photo or graphic illustration.

Fact sheet. Significant information about an organization in brief form; often statistical or historical.

Fourth estate. A reference to the press in its watchdog role over the three branches of a democratic society: executive, legislative, and judicial.

Headline writers. Reporters write news stories, but editors write the headlines. Headlines must capture the main thrust of a story in as few words as possible.

Lead. The first and most important sentence of a news story, whether it's print or broadcast.

News release. A planned piece of written information for the news media intended to relay information or create publicity.

Op-ed. The page opposite a newspaper's editorial page. Because op-ed pieces are located in the editorial section, they are considered opinions as opposed to objective news reporting.

Press kit. A package of promotional materials designed to gain the attention of a particular audience.

Public. A group, such as library users, whose members share certain characteristics, interests, and concerns.

Speaking off the record. When a reporter agrees that he or she will not use the information you provide, you are speaking "off the record." Unless you have the utmost trust in the reporter, don't do it.

Speaking on background. You and the reporter agree that the reporter may use the information but will not quote you or disclose you as the source.

Speaking on the record. Anything you say "on the record" can be quoted directly and attributed to you. Be safe; assume that everything you say is on the record.

Stakeholders. Another name for a group or public whose members share certain characteristics, interests, and concerns.

Talking points. Brief explanations that capture the core of the message you wish to convey.

Uncontrolled media. Mass media outlets—newspapers, television, radio, the Internet—that are not under the control of an organization. Uncontrolled media are generally perceived to be more objective and thus more credible.

FURTHER READING

Baskin, Otis, and Craig Aronoff. *Public Relations: The Profession and the Practice.* 4th ed. New York: McGraw-Hill, 1996.

Bivins, Thomas H. *Public Relations Writing: The Essentials of Style and Format.* 4th ed. Lincolnwood, Ill.: NTC/Contemporary, 1999.

Center, Allen H., Patrick Jackson, and Melvin L. Sharpe. *Public Relations Practices: Managerial Case Studies and Problems.* 6th ed. New York: Prentice Hall, 2002.

Cohn, Robin. *The PR Crisis Bible: How to Take Charge of the Media When All Hell Breaks Loose.* New York: St. Martin's, 2000.

Cutlip, Scott M., Allen H. Center, and Glen M. Broom. *Effective Public Relations.* 8th ed. New York: Prentice Hall, 1999.

Freestone, Julie, and Rudi Raab. *Disaster Preparedness: Simple Steps for Businesses.* Menlo Park, Calif.: Crisp, 1998.

Goldstein, Norm, editor. *Associated Press Stylebook and Briefing on Media Law.* Cambridge, Mass.: Perseus, 2002. Published annually.

Guth, David W., and Charles Marsh. *Public Relations: A Values-Driven Approach.* Needham Heights, Mass.: Allyn and Bacon, 2000.

Hendrix, Jerry A. *Public Relations Cases.* 5th ed. Belmont, Calif.: Wadsworth, 2000.

Henry, Rene A. *You'd Better Have a Hose If You Want to Put Out the Fire.* Windsor, Calif.: Gollywobbler, 2000.

Janis, Irving L. *Crucial Decisions: Leadership in Policymaking and Crisis Management.* New York: Free Press, 1989.

Kessler, Lauren, and Duncan McDonald. *When Words Collide.* 5th ed. Belmont, Calif.: Wadsworth, 1999.

Lukaszewski, James E. *Crisis Communication Planning Strategies: A Crisis Communication Management Workbook.* New York: Public Relations Society of America and Lukaszewski Group, 2000.

Mitroff, Ian I., and Christine M. Pearson. *Crisis Management: A Diagnostic Guide for Improving Your Organization's Crisis Preparedness.* San Francisco: Jossey-Bass, 1993.

Mitroff, Ian I., and Gus Anagnos, contributor. *Managing Crises Before They Happen; What Every Executive Needs to Know about Crisis Management.* New York: American Marketing Assn., 2001.

O'Hair, Dan, Gustav W. Friedrich, and Lynda Dee Dixon. *Strategic Communication in Business and the Professions.* 4th ed. Boston: Houghton Mifflin, 2002.

INDEX

American Library Association (ALA), 65
American Red Cross, 5
anthrax, 18–19, 57
areas of vulnerability, 35–42

building problems, 30

Columbine High School, 2
combating negative publicity, 58
communicating during a crisis
   immediacy, 53, 55
   messages with feeling, 52
   power of emotion, 52
   to-do list, 58
communications grid, 22
communications kit
   checklist, 10–11
   contact information, 8–12, 51
   fact sheet, 12
   gathering and maintaining crisis-ready information, 7–11
   to-do list, 12
community partners, 17
computer problems, 30
contact information, 8–12, 51
Cooper, Ginnie, 13
crisis aftermath
   celebration, 61
   debriefing, 61–62
   perception of public, 60
   post-crisis actions, 65
   preparing for next emergency, 63

restoring stakeholder trust, 62
sharing knowledge, 63
strengthening relationships with media, 62
thanking participants, 61
written narrative, 63
crisis communication
   how to speak, 52–58
   immediate responses, 53–57
   media log, 56–57
   plan, 4–5
   speaking out, 57–58
   successful scenario, 63–64
   to-do list, 58–59
   website, 56
crisis communications plan
   development 4–5
   elements, 5
   work in progress, 64–65
crisis communications team
   contact information, 14
   legal adviser, 17
   members, 13–17
   public relations manager, 15
   sample job description, 17
   spokesperson, 15, 18–19
   to-do list, 19
crisis management, 2–3
crisis potential
   annual library checkup, 26–29
   forecasting, 29–31
   organizing potential, 31–33

Index

crisis potential—*continued*
   to-do list, 33–34
   vulnerability checkup, 27–31
crisis scenarios, 28–31
crisis-ready information, 37–39

debriefing, 61–62
disseminating information, 54–58

emergencies, 4, 28–29
emotional response, 52–53
Exxon *Valdez*, 2, 18

financial problems, 31
Foley, Maria E., 63–64
forecasting emergencies, 29–31

gathering information, 53
George, Jennifer, 52
Giuliani, Rudolph, 19, 52–53

human resources director, 16

interviews, 49

Jennings, Peter, 52–53
job description sample, 16

Kennedy, John F. Jr., 63–64
Kirk, David, 20
Kissinger, Henry, 7

legal advisers, 16
library annual checkup, 26–29
library audience
   communicating with, 21–24
   identifying stakeholders, 20–21
library communications tools, 10, 22–24
library crisis reponse, 42
library spokesperson, 18
Long, Sarah, 26

man-made problems, 31
mass media, 44–51
Mateas, Margo M., 44
media log, 56–57
media problems, 31

media relationships
   during a crisis, 47–48
   news conferences, 50
   nurturing relationships, 45–47, 54
   restoring trust, 62
   talking to the press, 48–50
   to-do list, 50
   working with the media, 44–51, 62

natural disasters, 30
negative publicity, 58
news conferences, 50
news release sample, 39, 69

Office of Homeland Security, 57
one voice, 18–19
OSHA. *See* United States Department of Labor Occupational Safety and Health Administration

patron problems, 29
Pentagon, 1
Perelman Security Group, 1
positive media relationships
   before a crisis occurs, 44–45
   during a crisis, 47–48
post crisis, 60–65
post-crisis actions, 65
potential problems, 29–31
power of emotion
   messages with feeling, 52
pre-crisis preparations, 3–6
predicating problems, 29–31
preparation before crisis, 3
prepared statements, 37–39
press relations, 48–50
problem patrons, 29
public information officer, 18
public relations, 3–4

ready response
   contact information, 7–12
   preparation and practice, 35–36
   sample news release, 39
   talking points, 40–41
   to-do list, 42
   workplace violence, 36–37

Reeves, Tim, 1
Ridge, Tom, 1, 57–58

sample news release, 39, 69
September 11, 2001, 1, 5
Spaeth, Merrie, 60
spokesperson, 18
staff problems, 30
stakeholders
    communications grid, 22, 24
    constituency or public, 9
    definition, 9
    distributing information, 55
    educating, 24–25
    identifying, 20–21
    maintaining communications with, 21–25
    nurturing, 24
    restoring trust, 62
    to-do list, 25

talking points, 40–41, 43
team building, 13–17
telephone tree, 19
Thompson, Tommy, 19

United States Coast Guard, 63–65
United States Department of Labor
    Occupational Safety and Health Administration (OSHA), 1

voice of the library, 18
vulnerability audit, 27–31
vulnerable areas, 35–42

website information, 11, 46–47, 56
workplace violence, 1, 36–37
World Trade Center, 1, 15, 18

Jan Thenell is the retired director of public relations for the Multnomah County Library, based in Portland, Oregon. During her fourteen-year tenure, the library won three John Cotton Dana Library Public Relations Awards as well as the nationally acclaimed Silver Anvil Award from the public relations industry. Prior to being hired to set up a public relations department for the library, Thenell served on the press-communications staff of Oregon Governor Victor Atiyeh and, earlier, was a member of the administrative faculty of Southern Oregon University. She has a master's degree in journalism from the University of Oregon and is accredited by the Public Relations Society of America. A longtime library advocate who has served on the boards of libraries both small and large, she now consults in the public relations field and teaches in the communications department of Marylhurst University in Portland.

www.ingramcontent.com/pod-product-compliance
Lightning Source LLC
Chambersburg PA
CBHW031226170426
43191CB00030B/290